LATIN AMERICA

AND

ECONOMIC INTEGRATION

LATIN AMERICA AND ECONOMIC INTEGRATION

REGIONAL PLANNING FOR DEVELOPMENT

WALTER KRAUSE
AND
F. JOHN MATHIS

UNIVERSITY OF IOWA PRESS IOWA CITY

Library of Congress Catalog Card Number: 78–115458
University of Iowa Press, Iowa City, Iowa 52240

Printed in the United States of America.
ISBN 87745–003–X

CONTENTS

TABLES

WALTER KRAUSE is John F. Murray Professor of Economics at The University of Iowa. He received his Ph.D. from Harvard University in 1945. He previously taught at the University of Texas, Dartmouth College, and the University of California (UCR), and has been associated in various capacities since 1946 with U.S. government and international agencies, both in Washington and abroad. He has done extensive work in Latin America and relative to Latin America. His numerous books, monographs, and articles deal with economic development, international economics and business, and the Latin American economy. Among his books are *Economic Development, The International Economy, International Economics, The Economy of Latin America,* and *International Economics and Business* (with F. John Mathis).

F. JOHN MATHIS is Associate Professor of Economics, State University of New York at Brockport. He studied at the University of California (UCR) and received his Ph.D. in Economics from The University of Iowa. He previously taught at the University of Illinois at Chicago Circle, and has done extensive research in Latin America under auspices of the Pan American Union. He has been a frequent contributor to scholarly journals, and has authored books and monographs on economic development, international economics and business, and the Latin American economy. His books include *International Economics and Business* (with Walter Krause) and *Economic Integration in Latin America.*

FOREWORD

The contribution of Walter Krause and F. John Mathis in this focus upon economic cooperation in Latin America is an important step in diffusing understanding of the development needs of nations and peoples. Economic capability is fundamental to development regardless of variations in form and expression of modernization. The emergence of new contenders for a place in the world economy calls for structural readjustments and inventive solutions to permit, induce, and sustain growth. In the rhetoric of international policy, there is recognition of the necessity for economic cooperation to provide access to stable markets for the products of national economies. Beyond this, considerable agreement exists regarding how to proceed through any and all means to reduce trade barriers and coalesce regional trade areas, with beneficial freedom from constraints and with workable complementation agreements.

A fresh emphasis upon the potentialities of development through subregional common market areas is given by Professors Krause and Mathis. Internal and external constraints have slowed progress in the decade of the 1960s. A more realistic view is required of Latin America's need to sustain and stimulate trade, under favorable conditions, with the United States and other industrialized nations. Hopefully, recognition of this will be made in international agreements of the next decade.

The authors here provide analysis of progress, evaluation of vehicles of cooperation, and details of experience to date. Data, not available to readers elsewhere, are included in a Statistical Appendix, along with a thorough bibliography of related reference materials that scholars should find highly useful.

James Harris
Chairman
Graduate Program in Urban and Regional Planning
The University of Iowa

January 1970

LATIN AMERICA

PREFACE

This book, as its title *LATIN AMERICA AND ECONOMIC INTEGRATION: Regional Planning for Development* suggests, is about Latin America's plan to accelerate economic development through regional economic integration.

Much has occurred in Latin America in the use of regional economic integration as a means of developmental promotion. The decade of the 1950s had been one of extensive preparatory work. This was followed with the formal activation, at the outset of the 1960s, of two major integration organizations: the Central American Common Market and the Latin American Free Trade Association. More recently, prompted by a record of accomplishment alongside continuing unmet expectations, attention has turned to vastly expanded operational goals for the 1970s.

In this spirit, looking forward to the years ahead, the focus is now on movement to a fully *region-wide* common market—to the Latin American Common Market (LACM). The rationale for a LACM is simple. If benefits accrue from the economic integration of parts of Latin America (as presumed under integration activity heretofore), then even greater benefits promise to derive from the economic integration of the entire region.

As authors, we have published works previously, individually and jointly, that have treated at length earlier phases of the integration movement in Latin America. In the present volume, we have sought to carry these efforts forward by focusing directly on the latest phase: entry into the LACM. Our intent has been to produce a reasonably compact volume, placing our emphasis squarely on the current era and the future. Paralleling this emphasis, our primary concern has been with the major issues on hand and arising; the important policy questions posed by the new circumstances; and the implications generated in various respects because of actions occurring or contemplated. For the convenience of readers wishing to survey background materials bearing on the text, we have included documentary and statistical appendices, along with appropriate footnote references to specific information within them. Likewise, we have included a selective bibliography of the literature on Latin American economic integration.

We have had occasion earlier, through conferences and public lectures, to offer portions of the substantive content of this volume. The full content of what now appears was first offered by us in response to an invitation by Professor James Harris for our participation in a graduate seminar series, "Process and Problems of Development: Latin America," sponsored by the Department of Urban and Regional Planning, University of Iowa. We were able in that forum to point out that proponents view regional economic integration as the core element of "the plan" intended to assure development for Latin America; and that integration activity, so construed along multi-country lines, constitutes planning in a new form.

We wish to avail ourselves of this means to express our deep appreciation to Professor Harris for his invitation in the connection cited. Also, we wish to acknowledge our indebtedness to the California Institute of International Studies (CIIS) and its Executive Director, Professor Ronald Hilton of Stanford University, for the kind permission granted us to draw upon materials for our Chapter 3 that we had published earlier with CIIS. Similarly, we wish to thank the editors of the *Quarterly Review of Economics and Business* in reference to materials used in our Chapter 2.

Finally, a word about our division of labor. The manuscript is a joint effort, but with primary initial responsibility for Chapter 2 by Professor Mathis and for Chapter 4 by Professor Krause.

W. K.
F. J. M.

May 1, 1969

Chapter 1 / Latin America: Planning, Integration, and Development

To attempt to mould all [of Latin America] into a single nation, with but one bond to bind its parts each to each and each to all, is a grandiose concept.

Simón Bolívar

There is nothing so powerful as an idea whose time has arrived.

Anonymous

MEETING in "summit conference" in Punta del Este, Uruguay, during April 1967 under sponsorship of the Organization of American States (OAS), the "heads of state" of Latin America and the United States joined in approving an historic document, the "Declaration of the Presidents of America."[1] By terms of the agreement reached, the countries of Latin America, supported by the United States, stood committed to proceed with the launching of a region-wide "Latin American" common market. The target date set for actual initiation of the projected Latin American Common Market (LACM) was 1970, to be followed with action as necessary to turn all of Latin America into substantially a single economy by no later than 1985.

[1] Appraisal of the significance of the meeting was reflected in the tone of labels quickly attached: "Summit Conference," "Chiefs of State" meeting, etc. The formal sessions occurred during April 12–14, 1967. The resultant "Declaration of the Presidents of America"—excerpts of which appear in the Documents Appendix to this volume—received full approval from all OAS members (all countries of Latin America except Cuba, *plus the United States*).

A pronouncement of such magnitude obviously must have a considerable story associated with it. Certainly the event itself is triggered by what has gone before, and by an expectation of results to come. But, also, a multitude of questions are unleashed for the transition from mere goal to actual attainment. Let us, therefore, turn to this story—beginning with the major circumstances that had led to Punta del Este.

THE BACKGROUND

When Latin America broke politically free of Europe, the region fragmented into independent political entities roughly coinciding with what the ex-colonial powers had previously created for their own administrative and economic convenience. The newly-independent countries were both numerous and of varying size, strength, and influence. But, however much differing on some scores, all bore the imprint of a colonial heritage. Especially important, all were characterized by narrowly-based economies geared as much or more to the needs of external trade as to demands of domestic or regional gratification.

Simón Bolívar, recognizing the nature and limitations of the particular heritage, advanced an ideal: the goal of a unified Latin America stretching from the Rio Grande to Cape Horn. Often alluded to during succeeding decades by politicians and scholars alike, the goal nonetheless remained quite elusive as nationalism took ever deeper root within the compartmentalized entities of the region. Thus, Latin America continued in a traditional mold—*until,* during and after World War II, certain events intruded to shake the basic pattern.

The basic change that was then occurring was associated with the "Great Awakening." To increasing extent, concern came to be with "economic development"; political considerations, so important to Bolívar's thinking and to that of generations of his successors, lost ground to economic considerations as the realization dawned that, without economic adequacy, political nicety remains rather barren. But, interestingly, while many were convinced (or were becoming convinced) of "Latin America's" need for economic development, they continued to advocate supportive action along single-country lines—within the confines of the compartmentalized country-framework that prevailed.

In the new spirit of pro-development, numerous countries formulated "plans," believing that conscious direction on their part might assure them of results surpassing anthing likely to flow from chance alone. To the chagrin of every country, however, self-help consistently proved insufficient for expectations. And the outside help that had been hoped for did not materialize; the affluent United States, for example, was absorbed in other involvements[2] and so did not respond as many would have liked.

Though some economic gains were being realized, at least selectively, dissatisfaction was also mounting. There was impatience with the rate of development itself; and there was disenchantment with the extent of outside help. Under the circumstances, it was perhaps inevitable that responsible persons should look ever more sharply at how Latin Americans, proceeding in their own behalf, might do better for themselves. The particular "answer" that came to be interjected and that succeeded in capturing the popular imagination was "regional economic integration."

Spearheaded by the Economic Commission for Latin America (ECLA),[3] then under the headship of Raúl Prebisch,[4] the idea of regional economic integration represented a merging of a bit of

---

[2] Disposed to return to "normalcy" following World War II (as evidenced in a rapid demobilization), the United States soon was confronted with circumstances abroad that prompted expensive involvements: (1) Marshall Plan aid for Western Europe, and (2) special aid for certain underdeveloped regions, primarily in Asia, where strong communist pressures had arisen.

[3] Shortly after World War II, certain regional arrangements were introduced as affiliates of the United Nations: the Economic Commission for Latin America (ECLA), the Economic Commission for Asia and the Far East (ECAFE), etc. ECLA—with headquarters in Santiago, Chile—was envisaged as a "voice" for Latin America in particular specialized respects. Specifically, it was charged with a research and advisory function relative to economic and social problems of concern to the region.

[4] Raúl Prebish, Argentine by birth and professionally well known throughout Latin America even before becoming Secretary-General of ECLA, is responsible for numerous publications during his ECLA years. Major works during this period that summarize his views in their evolution include: United Nations, *The Economic Development of Latin America*, New York, 1950; "The Role of Commercial Policies in Underdeveloped Countries," *American Economic Review, Papers and Proceedings*, May 1959; and United Nations, *Towards a Dynamic Development Policy for Latin America*, New York, 1963. He is responsible also for United Nations, *Towards a New Trade Policy for Development*, New York, 1964, issued after his move to head the UNCTAD organization within the United Nations; this publication served as background for the famed "UNCTAD I" conference of 1964 at which a direct confrontation between all underdeveloped and all developed countries occurred on matters of trade and development.

Bolívar's thinking with that of the "infant industry" argument once invoked to sanction tariff protection. As propounded by Prebisch, meaningful development in Latin America was contingent on the realization of structural change—meaning a considerable acquisition of new industry. But, as he pointed out, scale of output being crucial in manufacturing, the basic context of development then had to be regional (multi-country), not single-country. In practical terms, there needed to be a movement to a "common market" in Latin America; unless the market area was enlarged to where it might sustain desired production and disposal, the necessary development could not ensue.

The decade of the 1950s was largely one of discussion and of clearing away roadblocks—political as much as economic—that beset ultimate action. As the decade neared its close, circumstances appeared particularly propitious (not only because of past preparatory work in Latin America, but because the United States had undergone a change of heart and was actually encouraging Latin America to proceed).[5] Thereupon, two new integration organizations were introduced in swift succession: in 1959, the Central American Common Market (CACM), linking five countries of Central America exclusive of Panama; and, in 1960, the Latin American Free Trade Association (LAFTA), initially linking seven countries (Argentina, Brazil, Chile, Mexico, Paraguay, Peru, and Uruguay) and later joined by four others (Bolivia, Colombia, Ecuador, and Venezuela).[6]

Thus, regional economic integration was on its way. Admittedly, with two organizations on hand, it was not the integration that advo-

---

[5] Events in Cuba, plus the poor reception accorded then Vice-President Nixon during his Latin American tour of 1958 (following a recession in the United States and depressed export levels in Latin America), triggered a reappraisal by this country of its posture toward Latin America. Drawing upon a list of proposals volunteered at the time by the then Brazilian President (Kubitschek) as the starting point for this reappraisal (a process referred to by Washington as "Operation Pan America"), the United States ended by embracing several of the ideas: the need in Latin America for regional economic integration (leading to a policy statement at least mildly supportive of such action); the advisability of a new regional development bank for Latin America (leading to support for creation of the Inter-American Development Bank); and so forth.

[6] A "free trade association," like a "common market," gives rise to a single multi-country market area within which goods can move about free of man-made barriers. But there is a technical difference between them in the sense that member countries under a "common market" agree to a uniform (common) external tariff on imports from outside the region, whereas member countries under a "free trade association" remain free to impose individual levels of duty on their imports from outside the region.

cates of a "fully unified" Latin America had urged. Yet, viewed in another sense, what had been ushered in stood as a sharp departure from the strictly national orientation of days past. Basic to all, the date was early; only time would tell what more, if anything, would evolve.

THE ROLE OF PLANNING

Accompanying the urge for economic development is a growing interest in development planning. Planning, of course, can take many forms; technically, even the decision not to plan constitutes *a* plan. More commonly, planning refers to a conscious attempt to mobilize and direct effort. The logic is that deliberateness can yield results not possible, or not probable as surely or as rapidly, in the absence of such deliberateness.

In Latin America, the years since World War II have been marked by much planning. Invariably, the approach has been on a single-country basis and has led to formal documents characterized by a certain preoccupation with precision methodology and a direct concern for no longer than the near-term future (2 to 5 years). Despite wide agreement on the need to plan, criticism of the plans that have emerged has been considerable. The criticism heard most frequently has centered not on the content of the plans, but on the implementation (or lack of it) of the plans. In essence, many observers seemingly have regarded the plans themselves to be at least substantively defensible, but then have gone on to deplore the lack of action, or the poor caliber of action, that followed from them.

Admittedly, a great deal can be said on the insufficiencies of implementation in planning.[7] But much might be said *also* about the content of plans. Especially this has been so since regional economic integration has come into its own. The point, very simply, is that the planning to be regarded as appropriate when regional integration is taken seriously is a different kind of planning than that appropriate when the focus is single-country in nature.

When regional economic integration is at issue, planning (at aggre-

[7] For a major work that surveys the planning efforts of many countries (member countries of the World Bank), and that offers considerable insight on the matter of implementation (conveying an indictment on this score), see Albert Waterston, *Development Planning: Lessons of Experience* (Baltimore: Johns Hopkins Press, 1965).

gate level) should have a regional (multi-country) focus, not a single-country focus. Unfortunately, both expertise and experience abound in reference to single-country planning, but not for regional planning.[8] The know-how and "feel" for regional planning—relative to both plan formulation and plan implementation—await more having happened during a further interval,[9] even while the need for them already exists.

Continuing on the matter of plan formulation, regional economic integration suggests a need for long-range planning (covering a time span longer than the traditional plan period of 2 to 5 years). With structural change an intended product of regional integration (as envisaged under the motivating rationale in the case of Latin America), and with such structural change of desired amount potentially realizable only over substantial time, the case for long-range planning becomes quite apparent. Unfortunately, the procedures appropriate to long-range planning are as yet at an immature stage and, moreover, do not appear to follow as a natural extension from the planning methodology associated with the traditional shorter-range plans.[10]

Concern with the type of plan(s) appropriate for Latin America *in the light of* regional economic integration is quite legitimate. Yet,

---

[8] Perusal of the major planning literature, including standard texts of recent vintage, reveals the single-country emphasis suggested. It is significant, however, that within Latin America, in keeping with the considerable interest in regional integration, serious attention is being directed to the "principles and practices" of regional planning. Evidence of this exists, for example, in the presence of the Institute for Latin American Integration (INTAL), created in 1965 as a subsidiary organization of the Inter-American Development Bank to carry out research, training, and advisory activities on integration.

[9] Illustrative of latent issues, should a "regional plan" be a single plan covering a number of countries? Or, should each country devise its own plan, subject to overall coordination during preparation and implementation? In either case, where does final authority lie when scope extends beyond individual countries?

[10] Planning of the shorter-range variety, especially should reliance during plan formulation be placed on precision techniques with the intent of impact optimization over the particular plan period (in terms of yearly per-capita income gain), can bias preference in action in favor of "squeezing the maximum from the prevailing production order" and against structural change (where considerations of short-term gain are frankly subordinated to the possibilities of greater-than-offsetting longer-term gain as a consequence of a *changed* production order). In effect, the conclusion suggested is that planning under conditions presupposing structural change merits being pursued either (a) in long-range terms or (b) in essentially policy terms (emphasizing "direction" over precision), *or* (c) in accordance with some combination of these two, hopefully with goodly attention to specific projects.

the fact remains that the very presence of regional integration as an active force *is* evidence of "a plan" of further sort—a super plan! In Latin America, accelerated economic development is widely desired; and, as many Latin Americans see it, regional economic integration comprises *the* most powerful means available to the countries of the region for promoting this development. Viewed in these terms, the "plan" at highest level is to prod development with integration effort, and to assume, pursuant to this, that other planning can afford to accommodate, reinforce, and supplement.

Implicit in the foregoing is a conviction that regional economic integration comprises the single most powerful means of developmental promotion available to Latin America. The reasoning that attaches—alluded to earlier in connection with the Prebisch (and ECLA) thesis—proceeds essentially as follows. For development of desired magnitude to become a reality, there must be substantially greater production (yielding added income and employment). The requisite production capacity necessitates investment (along with accompanying effort), itself motivated or deterred by the extent of likelihood of an adequate disposal of output. This disposal, in turn, hinges on the sufficiency of market outlets. It is at this juncture—relative to the matter of the market—that regional integration enters the picture. Regional integration brings into being a regional (multi-country) market area, accessible throughout from anywhere within. With access to the larger market area, (a) volume output becomes possible (especially important in manufacturing where the realization of economies of scale is essential for competitive costs, and where marked expansion is necessary to give meaning to needed structural change[11]) *because* (b) volume sales become possible (when the physical market is present and product prices are competitive).

Regional economic integration is thus viewed as yielding an environment under which the investment is induced that assures the development that is desired. The approach involved is both bold and potentially quite forceful, lending considerable credence to the cited appraisal of integration as *the* foremost lever of development. In comparison to "a plan" at this level, other planning along more customary

[11] The central case for structural change, involving industrial development, is that of a "new frontier" alongside the raw-materials sector, which offers relatively poor expansion prospects because of perverse demand conditions confronting product items.

lines does seem subsidiary, or does merit becoming supportive.[12]

As a plan form, regional integration appears, additionally, to have certain other attributes. Its focus is long-range, and its direct concern is the basic one of structural change. But, as an offset, one must recognize that in invoking regional integration as a lever of development, Latin America is embarking upon uncharted waters. The European experience (under the Common Market there) offers little that is readily transferable; under the developed conditions of Europe, the goal is "efficiency" rather than that of development. In effect, Latin America finds itself engaged in pioneering; its reliance on regional integration as an instrument of development is a "first" for it, and whatever happens there stands to be "a model" in the future for other underdeveloped regions considering avenues of possible developmental acceleration.

THE CURRENT JUNCTURE

As noted, by 1960 Latin America had two major organizations on the scene concerned with regional integration: CACM and LAFTA. During succeeding years, a considerable record accrued—some successes, some failures, many challenges. But, on balance, the record looked good enough and the outlook for the future promising enough that when the opportunity arose in Punta del Este (1967) to move ahead, toward a *single* region-wide "Latin American" common market, the assembled countries chose to endorse the step.

Since adoption of the "Declaration of the Presidents of America," work has been proceeding in Latin America—especially within and through LAFTA—preparatory to the formal shift to a LACM framework, projected per plan for 1970. The work has been neither easy nor routine, but the fact that it has continued has attested to a determination that may find its reward in the fulfillment of expectations.

In any event, the immediate years ahead appear crucial. Can the preparatory work being done prove adequate for what lies ahead? Can the difficult transition years following entry into a LACM be successfully weathered? What, actually, are the prospects for, or under, a LACM? And, success or failure, what are the logical implications of that which is occurring, or is likely to occur?

---

[12] Some forms of effort in regional integration are themselves supportive—for example, infrastructure projects of regional scope undertaken in support of production at or near the end-product stage.

In the sections that follow, these and other matters are explored. Chapter 2 surveys the progress toward a LACM and the major problems being encountered enroute. Thereafter (in Chapter 3), one problem—that of the status of the so-called "lesser developed" countries[13]—is singled out for special treatment because of the probability of its proving most troublesome of all. In a closing section (Chapter 4), speculation is advanced concerning the prospects and implications of the entire movement to, and under, a LACM.

---

[13] The term "lesser developed" has a special technical meaning in the case of Latin American regional economic integration. Admittedly some countries of Latin America are less developed than are others; however, "lesser developed," rather than the direct equivalent of "less developed," is more akin to the description inherent in the word "weaker." Under LAFTA, for example, the lesser developed countries are regarded as not only those that are least developed (i.e., have the lower per-capita income), but also those that are relatively weak on some scores quite beyond low per-capita income (e.g., have "insufficient market" conditions at home, like Venezuela, or have grave domestic problems of inflation or of a balance-of-payments nature, like Uruguay).

The reader may wish to examine the listing of countries in Table 1, and elsewhere, in the Statistical Appendix. According to current formal usage in the Latin American case, three countries are classed as "more developed": Argentina, Brazil, and Mexico. All other countries are classed as "lesser developed." But these "lesser developed" countries are, in turn, classed either as subject to "insufficient market" conditions or as being "relatively less developed."

Chapter 2 / The Latin American Common Market: Progress and Problems

Regional economic groupings, integration or other forms of economic co-operation should be promoted among developing countries as a means of expanding their . . . trade and encouraging their economic growth . . . .

United Nations Conference on Trade and Development, 1964

. . . Latin America has sounded a new keynote in regional relations . . . —the movement toward integration.

Felipe Herrera

Latin America, generally acknowledged as farther along developmentally than other major underdeveloped regions, has increasingly been looked to by countries in these other regions, as well as by countries in the developed category, as "a model" of developmental strategy and tactics. Especially important in this respect during recent times has been Latin America's innovative effort in invoking regional economic integration—a movement toward, and to, a regional common market—as a basic lever of developmental promotion.

The present chapter is about the Latin American common market movement—specifically, about (a) the progress being made on a Latin American Common Market (LACM), and (b) the problems that are present and arising to encumber this progress and that demand amelioration, if not full resolution, for realization of expected success.

FROM PAST TO PRESENT

The era of World War II was one in Latin America during which thoughts of economic development took serious hold. Thereafter, in the wake of such thoughts, various development strategies were contemplated and several were activated. Invariably, however, disappointment characterized reaction as effective developmental impact seemed to lag. Against this background, Latin America in due course moved to yet another developmental approach: economic integration. In swift succession, two integration organizations of special note were instituted: in 1959, the Central American Common Market (CACM), embracing five countries of Central America outside Panama, and, in 1960, the Latin American Free Trade Association (LAFTA), linking the countries of South America[1] and Mexico. It was in terms of effort associated with these new organizations—expecially LAFTA, claiming the larger countries and covering, *in toto,* over 90 percent of the entire area, population, and GNP of the region—that Latin America henceforth envisaged the fundamental thrust of its developmental aspirations.[2]

LAFTA, the dominant organization, was ushered in by acceptance of the Treaty of Montevideo.[3] The underlying rationale was that of developmental promotion within the region by unleashing the inducements inherent in the process of creating a single multi-country market entity. The specific technique held central for implementation was that of a gradual removal of barriers to intrazonal trade—involving, in essence, a gradual movement toward a "Latin American" common market. Pursuant to these basic qualities, the governing Treaty, a concise document leaning to considerable flexibility, outlined accompanying features:

(1) A program of trade liberalization spanning 12 years, intended to free items of intrazonal trade of all restriction by member countries. Such trade items were classed in two categories for purposes of liberalization procedure: (a) a "National List" of items toward which members agreed on annual reductions of duty and/or other restriction, and (b) a "Common List" of items of current trade to be fully freed of restriction, in any event, by no later than 1973.

[1] All except the Guianas, once Bolivia, Colombia, Ecuador, and Venezuela had joined the initial membership.

[2] For supporting data, the reader is referred again to Table 1 in the Statistical Appendix; also to Table 2, which highlights further the relative strength of the LAFTA area and of particular member countries.

[3] A convenient source for the text of the Treaty of Montevideo is Sidney Dell, *A Latin American Common Market?* (New York: Oxford University Press, 1966), app. II:B, pp. 228–56.

(2) The goal of expanded intrazonal trade and of greater economic complementarity within the region.
(3) Retention of a most-favored-nation clause, assuring the extension of liberalization benefits to all member countries.
(4) Provision for internal taxation on imports no less favorable than that accorded similar national products.
(5) Retention of "escape clauses," enabling a country to restrict importation whenever a given product "threatens" the national economy.
(6) Special provisions on behalf of agriculture.
(7) Special provisions aimed at allaying "lesser developed" member countries of fears of economic inundation within a regional context.
(8) Institutions and administrative organs: a Conference of Contracting Parties and Executive Committee, an intrazonal payments system, and a Council of Ministers to head LAFTA beginning in 1966.

Though elements of success could be pointed to during the ensuing years (in investment, in trade, and in tariff liberalization itself), not all was clear gain. Aside from a growing feeling of disappointment with the overall pace of progress, specific weaknesses were showing up. For example, intrazonal trade within LAFTA as a percentage of the total foreign trade of member countries, which had risen from 6 percent in 1961 to about 12 percent by 1965, thereafter began to decline, standing at but 10 percent in 1967.[4] Again, tariff concessions in terms of the National List, gratifyingly great during early years, subsequently began to decrease in number with each year;[5] moreover, a rising proportion of concessions actually granted were found to pertain to items only rarely traded or only decreasingly available for trade.[6]

The foregoing nonetheless, sentiment for a meaningful common market movement continued, and even intensified. It was in this context of persistent expectation alongside lagging realization that, dur-

---

[4] For background data on LAFTA trade, see Table 3 in the Statistical Appendix.

[5] See Table 4, Statistical Appendix.

[6] Illustrative of this, information contained in Table 5, Statistical Appendix, reveals that already by 1964 the cited trend was much in evidence. Continuing information along these lines is contained in LAFTA (Comite Ejecutivo Permanente), *El Comercio Exterior de la ALALC* (CEP/Repartido 1161), Montevideo, 1969, pp. 28–32.

ing April 1967 at an OAS-sponsored "heads of state" meeting in Punta del Este, the decision was reached (in the form of the "Declaration of the Presidents of America," subscribed to by the United States in company of the countries of Latin America) to support the establishment of a fully region-wide Latin American common market (LACM), the movement toward such to be substantially completed by no later than 1985. The expressed intent was to move toward the full LACM by building upon the base already on hand in LAFTA plus CACM (but especially LAFTA). The procedures envisaged were, in the main, two in number: (a) continued trade liberalization and (b) attention to multinational projects.

Thereafter, efforts were initiated to implement the decision reached at Punta del Este. Unfortunately, early efforts unmistakably pointed to the presence of basic impediments. Illustrative of what was to beset the movement toward a LACM, two specific showdowns quickly emerged. In August 1967 in Asunción at the annual meeting of LAFTA's Council of Ministers, marking the first major attempt by Latin Americans to proceed with implementation, the Ministers encountered negotiation problems attributable to conflicts of interest rooted in the great differences in economic structures of the member countries.[7] In much the same vein, the Seventh Annual Conference

[7] The term "economic structure," as used here, refers to a country's general level of economic development or level of living, and encompasses the extent of industrialization, size of market, and degree of transportation and communications development. As evidenced by basic data in Tables 1 and 2, Statistical Appendix, the economies of Latin America currently vary widely in economic structure, so defined. With such diversity on hand, "conflicts of interest" are prone to emerge to complicate negotiations between countries—as, indeed, proved to be the case during the cited Asunción meeting. The dominant source of difficulty there was rooted in the belief that closer economic contact between countries (inherent in freer trade) tends to foster unequal rates of development among dissimilar countries, thereby actually intensifying the already-existing inequalities.

The matter of diversity is of interest, too, for reasons of insight into ongoing discussions among professional economists. Theoreticians frequently argue that integration effort is most likely to contribute to trade creation when the participating countries are economically diverse. However, something different may well pertain when the countries involved are underdeveloped (albeit to varying degree)—as clearly pointed out by Sidney Dell in *A Latin American Common Market?*, especially pp. 15–34. Specifically, the Latin American countries here at issue are diverse in terms of their relative levels of development (or underdevelopment), not in terms of their existing trade structures (which are very similar, emphasizing primary-products exports). Additionally, confusion—from a theoretical standpoint—arises because the traditional case for regional integration has been based on its static effects with respect to trade creation and

of LAFTA, meeting later during 1967, encountered negotiation difficulties relative to the Common List; the conferees proved unable to complete the requirements of the second Common List as disagreement surfaced over the inclusion of wheat and petroleum, products that together were accounting for over 25 percent of current intrazonal trade.

With the passage of but little time, realization became fairly widespread that *many* problems were certain to be involved in movement to a full-scale LACM—not only problems rooted in narrow conflicts of interest, but other problems, more general in scope, as well. Increasingly, talk was of the need to identify the major problems and to "think through" ways of contending with them. As came to be stated, the interim period preceding 1970, when formal embarkation on LACM measures was scheduled to occur, should aptly be regarded as one of serious preparation, brooking no delay and not to be minimized in importance.

THE PROBLEMS

Thus, the current era has been one of preparation for the action that is expected to follow. Indeed, understanding has come to exist that the major challenges will likely not strike until 1970, or after. Accordingly, preparation, in the minds of many, has come to mean a preparedness to interject counter-action *when and as* specific need arises during the course of a quite uncertain future.

Obviously, the likelihood of the problems in question can be circumvented simply by not proceeding with contemplated action. The governing thought, however, is that the common market movement, though fraught with problems, is indispensable for reasons of development—indeed, is already at the irreversible point.

Turning to the challenges confronting movement into a LACM, three major problem areas are readily identifiable: structural, financial, and administrative. Stated in minimal terms, the prospects for successful entry into a LACM depend on the adequacy of response to these problems.

---

trade diversion, whereas the underdeveloped countries have a natural and legitimate concern with the dynamic effects on the rate of growth. For them, integration represents a technique to use to *achieve* economic development, in which context intrazonal trade creation comprises only one element.

16

STRUCTURAL

Among the problems labeled here as "structural," two are paramount: (a) the problem of how to elicit full cooperation from widely-differing countries likely, under normal circumstances, to benefit in widely-differing degree, and (b) the problem of how to assure an appropriate complement of infrastructure, particularly as respects transportation and communications.

(1) *Economic disparity*. The countries of Latin America involved in the formation of a LACM present a broad spectrum: in size and physical characteristics; in current levels of per-capita income; and in terms of present stage of development.[8] Given such differences, a built-in problem is at hand. For a fully "Latin American" common market to come into being, *all* countries of the region must participate. Yet, with the diversity that prevails, not every country can blandly be assumed as likely to benefit to equal extent. Specifically, the competition generated under integration stands to favor the "stronger" countries over the "weaker" countries. The natural inclination, therefore, is for the weaker countries to resist (as nationalism and interpretations of self-interest constrict the attractiveness of near-amalgamation).

The challenge, of course, is to find ways to induce all countries, including the weaker countries (generally referred to, in a Latin American context, as the relatively "lesser developed" countries), to *want to* go along with integration; indeed, to find ways to induce their untrammeled cooperation *without,* at the same time, unduly jeopardizing the aggregate benefit potentially derivable under the integration process itself. The "answer" to reconciliation in the foregoing conflict between the lesser developed countries and those that are "more developed" lies with the pace of the integration process, the extent of integration, and the distribution of its benefits. The first two of these points are related directly to the third—in reference to which, in turn, essentially two approaches prevail: an equal distribution of benefit, *or* a granting of greater-than-proportional benefit to the lesser developed countries. In *either* case, special action appears needed for assurance of the desired distribution—without which results are envisaged that are untenable for certain countries, thereby dissuading them from membership or cooperation. The relevant

[8] See again Tables 1 and 2, Statistical Appendix.

question, therefore, becomes the following: *What* can be done to create a tenable basis for membership or cooperation?

The problem never confronted the CACM area in the way it did the LAFTA area; the CACM countries were all roughly similar (all lesser developed), whereas the LAFTA countries varied widely. Indeed, the problem for LAFTA was anticipated from the outset. The Treaty of Montevideo expressly recognized the special status of the lesser developed countries, and provided special measures for routing assured benefit to them. Subsequent resolutions went farther, providing for additional measures of benefit diffusion, for additional safeguards against possible loss, and, also, for further study of the entire matter by established groups in anticipation of yet other actions of amelioration. In general, the accepted principle throughout has been one of preferential treatment in trade and in technical and financial assistance for the lesser developed countries, to the extent required, in the interests of an "equitable distribution" of the gains potentially realizable under integration.

With the events of 1967, projecting a movement from a CACM-LAFTA structure to a full LACM structure, expectation has been that of an intensification of the problem of "economic disparity and benefit diffusion." Whatever the extent of the problem under LAFTA, it could only prove more severe under a LACM when the CACM countries, and the small countries currently remaining non-affiliated, are also thrust into close association with members like Argentina, Brazil, and Mexico. Though comment has proceeded in terms of "building on a CACM-LAFTA base," sheer size has forced the role of "core area and organization" upon LAFTA. Special directives have made clear the particular responsibility of LAFTA in the conversion to a common market, in the activation of a system of programmed elimination of duties and other non-tariff restrictions, in the formulation of a common external tariff, and in the evolution of guidelines for member countries apropos the coordination of national economic policies and the harmonization of national legal provisions.

As matters stand, many resolutions have been passed and many others are being studied and readied, within and outside LAFTA—but few have been implemented that are truly germane to the major task of physical transition to a full LACM. The current era has been one of preparation more than of actual implementation; indeed, formal entry into a LACM has been alluded to, both under the "Declaration of the Presidents of America" and in connection with supplementary activity subsequently, in terms of 1970 as a target date. Despite the early stage of direct implementation, however, there has been unmistakable progress in the realm of assessing what major operational features are already present that can be viewed, and used, as "steppingstones" in the course of moving to a LACM. Importantly, the framework of LAFTA, particularly, has given rise to at least three such elements: principles and procedures of tariff negotiation, the technique of complementation agreements, and the tactic of subregional integration. All, interestingly enough, had evolved in the context of resolving the dilemma of the lesser developed countries under past integration effort—and all currently hold a relevance in this same respect as attention turns to a LACM.

Relative to tariffs, LAFTA's immediate goal had been their gradual elimination, along with the elimination of other like barriers, in the interests thereby of expanding national markets and intrazonal trade. To be sure, significance was attached, as well, to supplementary devices, such as a closer coordination of regional planning—though, for all intents and purposes, the main thrust of effort lay with tariffs.

In practice, three principal tariff-cutting mechanisms became focal: the National List, the Common List, and complementation agreements. In terms of the National List, special concessions have been extended certain lesser developed countries (as in the case of Bolivia, Ecuador, and Paraguay), relieving them of obligation to comply with the 8 percent annual duty reduction specified by the Treaty (even as other member countries have continued with such reductions and assent, as well, to additional exclusive concessions). Throughout, LAFTA has demonstrated an ability to meet the requirements posed as minimal under the National List—though, in doing so, forcing problems that have grown with each passing year.

Illustrative of mounting difficulty apropos the National List, momentum for follow-up action on recommendations for concessions, customarily stemming from "industrial sector" meetings, has waned; despite a trend to rely more heavily on the recommendations of sectoral meetings, the number of concessions actually approved from among those recommended has been decreasing steadily. Also, certain major commodity categories have not proven particularly amenable to concessions; the category of agricultural and metal products, accounting for some 70 percent of intra-LAFTA trade, has provided about one-fourth of all concessions, whereas the manufactures category (primarily chemicals, machinery, and equipment), accounting for only about 20 percent of intra-LAFTA trade, has provided over one-half of all concessions.[9] Further, no direct relation has proven evident between costs involved in granting concessions and benefits of stimulus for increased industry through greater intra-regional trade; according to accumulating data, the trade advantage has been moving in favor of the more developed countries at the expense of the relatively less developed countries[10] (with in-between countries, sometimes classed as having "insufficient market" status, approximately holding their own)[11]—despite avowed intentions to attain contrary results.

Under the Common List, tariff concessions are computed on a percentage basis. As a result, countries with high export-import dependence—the relatively less developed countries—stand to be affected most; indeed, such impact could prove severe if, as initially scheduled to occur by 1973, all barriers to intrazonal trade are removed—certainly so if, during the interim, these countries fail to achieve significant diversification to alter their traditionally weak competitive position. Ongoing operations relative to the Common List present a mixed picture; though the first Common List gained ready approval, the second Common List, set for 1967, failed to win acceptance on schedule—in fact, continued dormant even as the 1970 date for the third Common List fast approached. Inherent difficulties stem from emphasis on items of current trade to the virtual exclusion of items not yet in being for active trade; and from emphasis on an array of items not truly central to Latin American trade. Relative to the latter, little attention is accorded agricultural items, a troublesome area under the Common List; indeed, general hesitancy appears to characterize the approach to agricultural items as evidenced by the decision, reached fairly early, to delay consideration of tariff treat-

[9] For a citation on applicable reference material, refer to fn. 6.

[10] As used here, "less developed" differs from "lesser developed" in the sense that the relatively less developed countries comprise but a part of those classed as lesser developed; a statement on the distinction appears in Chapter 1 (fn. 13).

[11] Though factors beyond tariff concessions admittedly also affect trade, it is revealing to note disparities such as a percentage increase in Mexico's intrazonal trade (exports and also imports) roughly five times as great, during 1960–67, as that recorded in, say, Ecuador, despite the granting by each of roughly similar percentages of total intrazonal tariff concessions. Extensive data on the direction of trade flows, and on modifications in direction, appear in Tables 6 and 7, Statistical Appendix.

ment of certain agricultural items beyond the 1973 deadline initially indicated as the outside date for final removal of barriers.

In order to lessen the difficulty typically encountered in trade liberalization, and to speed progress generally, one suggestion, increasingly heard, is to replace negotiation on a country-by-country and item-by-item basis with (a) negotiation by categories of goods and groups of countries, coupled with (b) a system of automatic tariff reductions, applicable either to all countries or to groups of countries. Aside from this, need exists for an approach that can lead to a reduction, or removal, of the region's non-tariff barriers, already extensive and continuing to proliferate. Though both of the foregoing matters have been brought before the Council of Ministers, remedial action remains in the future in the wake of a decision to undertake "further study."

A third approach to tariff liberalization (and, concurrently, the second among our previously-cited steppingstones toward a LACM) pertains to complementation agreements—arrangements to channel investment to particular locales, including the lesser developed countries with their small markets, by dividing production facets, or the production sequence itself, among two or more countries. The lesser developed countries are generally favorably inclined to participation in complementation agreements, viewing such arrangements as a possible way of assuring themselves of involvement in industrial development that might otherwise be centered almost entirely in the more developed countries. Unfortunately, only few agreements are currently in effect (despite the passage of some years) and, among those on hand, coverage applies basically to more developed countries, not a linkage between them and lesser developed countries.[12] The reason for few complementation agreements rests with technical problems anticipated in administration, contributing to an otherwise already-massive task at issue in their organization. Yet, results under existing complementation agreements indicate definite trade gains in relevant products between participating countries—suggesting that the technique is a hopeful one that merits further consideration for inducing cooperation by countries normally inclined to feel themselves somewhat outside the main stream of things.[13]

---

[12] Information on complementation agreements in force—industry at issue, participating countries, time of activation of agreement, etc.—is summarized in Table 8, Statistical Appendix.

[13] For supporting data, see Table 9, Statistical Appendix.

The third major steppingstone toward a LACM is subregional integration—under which two or more countries, situated somewhat less advantageously than the most advanced countries of the region, undertake to promote integration within their immediate zone in anticipation of an upgrading there that will facilitate full integration within the greater zone at some point during the near-term future. Gaining attention as a possible transitional measure to help ready lesser developed countries for general contact, subregional integration in Latin America dates, in practice, from 1964—at which time preliminary discussion commenced relative to formation, within operational terms of the Treaty of Montevideo, of an Andean Subregional Group.

Admittedly, advantages can be claimed for subregional integration. In the case of the Andean Group, for example, the countries concerned are not as advanced as are certain other LAFTA (or LACM) members such as Argentina, Brazil, or Mexico. If thrust into the greater context without further ado, the probability exists of untenable competition and disproportionately low benefit from contact. However, if "prepared" for such contact by means of semi-insulation (and accompanying self-directed effort) during a preliminary period, the likelihood is enhanced that eventual contact not only can be endured, but be looked forward to in terms of an assured sharing of resultant advantage.

Nonetheless, a counter-argument against subregional integration can also be advanced—one that merits recognition, if only for reasons that awareness can possibly help to preclude certain adverse side-effects from becoming fact. As some critics suggest, the semi-insulation of subregional integration risks the division of Latin America into autonomous economic blocs which, once on hand, can make eventual reunification into a single economic bloc well-nigh impossible.

Thus, there have been two basic views—pro and con—about subregional integration. In any event, LAFTA has responded by endorsing subregional integration whenever, avowedly, such has promised to conform to generalized guidelines (outlined by LAFTA). The premise has been that, if care is taken, the "good" from subregional integration can be captured without necessarily also having to incur the "bad." In fact, the premise has been that subregional integration lends itself in a way so as to qualify as more than just another steppingstone; that it can prove to be *the* foremost lever at LAFTA's command in helping disadvantaged countries to ease into a true LACM association.

Though further courses of action of major importance to economic integration may evolve in days ahead, the three that we have cited—but subregional integration, in particular—appear likely to continue as key elements in facilitating the establishment of a LACM. A central point of relevance in all of the foregoing is that the lesser developed countries are tempted to resist cooperation, and thereby to thwart movement to a full LACM, *unless* they are accorded some measure of reassurance to allay certain gnawing fears. The primary source of such reassurance thus far rests with the cited steppingstones; specifically, it is in terms of them—in assuring all countries, including especially the lesser developed countries, of identifiable benefits while, at the same time, avoiding negation or undue deterrence of over-all developmental progress—that prospect lies for the cooperation essential to meaningful integration. Of course, the prospect alluded to is truly bright only if the existing organizational framework proves adequate to the task of minimizing failure, as well as of pushing advantage, as respects each of the major steppingstones.

(2) *Transportation and communications.* Success in a common market movement presumes that the integration process extends, also, to facets of infrastructure—particularly to transportation and communications. In this spirit, interestingly enough, the "Declaration of the Presidents of America" focuses heavily upon infrastructure as a component (or lever) of integration.

Relative to transportation and communications facilities, over-all status in Latin America currently is that of general inadequacy, either for development or for integration, per se. To illustrate with transportation, facilities prevailing within given countries reflect an orientation to foreign trade, not domestic trade (routes run to the coast rather than serving as parts of a national network); indeed, the orientation is to distant foreign trade, not to foreign trade of regional scope (with contiguous countries or even with non-contiguous countries elsewhere within Latin America).

Unfortunately, though transportation is generally inadequate, an appropriate upgrading is not easy to come by. Physical obstacles, rooted in geography, are present: vast distances, mountainous terrain, dense jungles, etc. And present, also, are financial obstacles; to do what is needed entails high cost (and raises problems of distribution of cost, as well), and such cost comes at a time when the financial demands of development are rising on many fronts.

To be sure, pro-development action (of regional scope) on behalf of transportation is occurring; major cases include remaining linkages in the Pan American Highway and the considerable effort associated with construction of the so-called Marginal Highway of the Jungle, traversing hitherto unopened areas east of the Andes. And, what can be said of transportation can also be said of communications; the problems are great, but action is occurring—as, for example, in effort to develop a regional telecommunications system. However, alongside such ongoing activity, the accurate assessment at the current juncture must be that a great deal remains to be done before "adequate" regional transportation and communications systems can be regarded as on hand.

FINANCIAL

Alongside challenges in the structural realm, problems of a financial nature also beset Latin America in its common market movement. Especially important in this connection are matters such as (a) access to requisite capital, (b) settlement of international accounts, and (c) inflation (and currency instability).

(1) *Financing for integration.* The integration effort that is intended to yield a common market is costly, both in material resources and in monetary commitments (national currency and foreign exchange). Unfortunately, Latin America, underdeveloped throughout but with considerable regional variation, has limits in the means—particularly monetary means—that it can hope to bring to bear. It is important, therefore, that careful attention be given to the mobilization of such means as are available and to their eventual placement and utilization.

In terms of indigenous financing, it is significant that at the very time that new activities, including new multinational projects, are being undertaken, the economic base from which the supportive financing is expected to come is itself undergoing change. To be precise, the countries of the region, traditionally heavily reliant upon customs receipts in the generation of governmental financing, are finding that the diminution of intrazonal tariff barriers under the integration movement has the effect of depriving their governments of substantial amounts of customary revenue—thereafter no longer available for developmental-type outlays. The result is that the countries of Latin America are obliged to consider certain revisions in their revenue structures (ostensibly toward income and wealth taxation) at the same time as they plan new investment outlays of a pro-integration type.

In terms of external capital, the need for added inflows suggests the wisdom of a "united front" approach to capital attraction. Instead of widely-varying investment-inducement provisions among the countries, a preferable line of attack involves coordination to achieve substantial uniformity (thereby avoiding mutually-destructive competitiveness)—coupled, hopefully, with attention to (a) shadings of difference geared to take into account the special status of lesser developed countries and (b) the fostering of an over-all environment conducive to a relatively free flow of capital among the countries.

Relative to both domestic and foreign facets, it appears desirable, further, that incentive aspects of financing be considered. More is involved than simply the assembly of funds and their formal routing thereafter. Taxation can be patterned to induce investment (whatever the source of funds) and to prod the tempo of economic activity generally; and the same can be said of investment provisions apropos external capital, including provisions covering remissions policy.

To generalize, an appropriate institutional framework is essential to assure that funds—public and private, indigenous and external—will find their way into those forms of investment upon which economic development hinges. Such an institutional framework, traditionally the responsibility of individual governments, becomes very much a regional consideration when development along regional lines is the goal. To this end, it is important that there be coordination among countries of the region, quite apart from the advisability of having, also, regional agencies attune to regional needs, with resources in meaningful amount at their disposal.

In this vein, the Inter-American Development Bank (IDB) was initiated in 1959, becoming Latin America's primary multilateral instrument for the channeling of financial and technical resources for individual-country and collective growth. Alluded to colloquially as the "Bank for Integration," IDB has undertaken to systematize varied activities on behalf of integration, in due course adding two subsidiary instrumentalities: (1) in 1965, the Institute for Latin American Integration (to carry out research, training, and advisory activities on integration), and (2) in 1966, the Preinvestment Fund for Latin American Integration (to arrange and finance preinvestment studies related to multinational and other projects likely to contribute to the acceleration of integration). Whatever else may be claimed for IDB, the assembly and distribution of funds under it, as well as its activity in related realms, has—on balance—favored the relatively less developed and "insufficient market" countries.[14]

(2) *Settlement of balances.* The presence of a regional trading and financial network (one, in fact, that is growing, as contemplated under Latin America's common market movement) presupposes the unlikelihood of an exact balancing of debits and credits in accounts between countries, certainly not during short-run periods. But uncleared balances must be dealt with in some way lest, in the absence of an alternative to the contrary, countries succumb to the simple process of contraction as the means for achieving balance (at some lower level of transactions). Indeed, however significant the matter of settlement of balances within strictly a regional context, a further complicating factor in the case of Latin America is that all the countries are typically short of quality foreign exchange (dollars, pounds, etc.)—and are, for that reason, quite reluctant to part with such foreign exchange in any settlement of uncleared regional balances.

Given the foregoing, Latin America, as the push toward a LACM proceeds, stands in need of a workable system for settling accounts multilaterally. Desirably, the system should (a) prove conducive to a high, and growing, volume of commercial and financial transactions

---

[14] Total loan volume has been heavily on behalf of the more developed countries (Argentina, Brazil, and Mexico), an expected result when account is taken of the relative size of these countries. Viewing loan volume on a *per-capita* basis, however, the lesser developed countries have fared far more favorably as beneficiaries. Loans approved by 1965, for example, revealed a per-capita distribution as follows among more developed countries: Argentina, \$6.39; Brazil, \$2.99; and Mexico, \$3.25. This contrasted with a per-capita distribution as follows among some of the lesser developed countries: Costa Rica, \$19.31; Nicaragua, \$17.73; and Paraguay, \$16.68. The general pattern, on a per-capita basis, has been that of greater assistance for the lesser developed countries, whether classed as relatively less developed or as having "insufficient market" status. Indeed, the trend in this direction has sharpened over time, aided in part by the availability for allocation of funds from the Social Progress Trust Fund, administered by IDB under the Alliance for Progress program.

Since national resources subscribed to IDB come heavily from the more developed countries, and then are allotted to greater-than-average extent to lesser developed countries, the effect is that of some amount of redistribution of capital resources within Latin America. This impact, present and even accelerating, appears quite in keeping with IDB's designation of itself as the "Bank for Integration."

between countries, free of pressure for contraction; (b) foster credit and financing links between countries; and (c) effect settlement of balances between countries without, in the process, unduly tying up scarce foreign exchange. What is described is, in effect, an arrangement that provides the services of a clearing house within the general framework of a zonal payments system.

Though no general clearing arrangement has yet evolved, a partial arrangement under LAFTA, with the Central Bank of Peru designated as central clearing agent, has been established. Under it, a number of bilateral sub-agreements have been negotiated, providing procedures and funds for facilitating multilateral transfers; the record in action, as one might expect, has been that the more developed countries show up as the creditor countries.[15] More recently, arrangements have been made to authorize non-LAFTA members to participate in the system of compensation.

(3) *Inflation and currency instability.* The fact that some countries of Latin America are subject to considerable inflation,[16] and that these or other countries are subject, also, to currency instability,[17] poses a problem under the common market movement—as evidenced in experience under LAFTA. With the price structures of individual countries changing at differing rates, the pattern of production and trade and the investment design itself come to be influenced *because* of price relationships external to circumstances normally relied upon as an index of relative efficiency. Unfortunately, an immediate effect is that investment, production, and trade are all thereby made somewhat more risky—an effect not in keeping with the over-all goal under integration of lending encouragement at each point in the sequence.

Standing short of centralized authority over all countries to assure uniformity of end price structures, a reasonable approach to the problem is to strive among participating countries for an element of coordination in their monetary and fiscal policies in the hope of holding disparities to at least manageable proportions. In that way, the threat of a choking off of investment, production, and trade because of disparities can be lessened; and, additionally, a great bur-

---

[15] See Table 10, Statistical Appendix.

[16] For supporting information, see Table 11, Statistical Appendix.

[17] Table 12, Statistical Appendix, contains data on recent values, *in terms of* the U.S. dollar, of various Latin American currencies. Present are examples of stability; gradual value erosion; and drastic revaluation on occasion (e.g., Brazil).

den can be removed from any regional clearance arrangements that exist. To date, however, this course of action remains largely a matter of discussion.

While implications abound for regional economic activity, the widespread inflation and currency erosion of Latin America entails implications, also, for economic relationships vis-a-vis the rest of the world. Certainly, foreign investment within the region by distant investors is subject to added risk; to worry over unpredictable trade relationships is added the worry of repatriation status following some future devaluation. Similarly, export prospects outside the region are thereby affected. Basic raw materials sell at world prices, and production in their case proceeds in this light; but some forms of output, such as newly-emerging manufactures, are extremely sensitive to prevailing price relationships. Thus, the price and currency positions of countries of the region become a matter for concern not only within Latin America, but *also* in relationships with countries outside Latin America.

ADMINISTRATIVE

Finally, there are administrative problems, in the nature of institutional and executive shortcomings, to beset integration effort. Already well recognized via LAFTA experience, these problems are of a type likely to continue—at least in principle if not in precisely identical form—as movement proceeds into a LACM.

(1) *Private and public.* Recognition prevails on the need in a common market movement of a proper response not only from governments, but from the private sector in the various countries, as well; for example, LAFTA has relied heavily on "sectoral meetings" in the belief that the private sector should play an important role in policy formulation—basically because the end results of implementation are expected to derive in great part from the private sector. Of course, while the proper atmosphere may be a necessary condition for the hoped-for response by private enterprise apropos regional development, such is not also to conclude that what is hoped for will automatically follow. Illustrative of what is at issue, added costs are likely to ensue, at least in an initial sense, as private enterprise attempts to respond to the needs and opportunities of an emerging regional market; costs arise in the training of labor for new tasks, in the course of experimentation on "best" scale of operations, in the

process of product development and the organization of distribution channels, etc. The bright side of the picture is that a successful hurdling of initial blocks, if actually resulting, can usher in a situation in which the servicing of a regional market on a profitable basis and the realization of economies of scale reinforce one another.

As with private enterprise, what happens with integration via the public sector depends on authority, and on the responsible exercise of this authority in the initiation and implementation of action. Relative to the requisite authority, it is well to realize that integration in Latin America is as much a political matter as an economic one; and that, as respects action, an inducement approach may prove as advantageous as compulsion, or even more so. Awaiting attention in this spirit, certain major administrative problems are confronting LAFTA in the movement toward, and to, a full LACM: the coordination of basic national policies and plans in the interests of achieving what is tantamount to long-range regional planning, especially long-range regional *investment* planning; the practice of negotiation on a regional basis with external countries, rather than, as traditionally, on a bilateral basis; and the implementation of a system of settlement between member countries of problems or disputes when such are triggered by economic self-interest or political-military rivalry.

In either case, be the concern with the private sector or the public sector, integration leadership needs to be up to the task. On this score, room remains for the evolution of greater certainty of direction and, very importantly, a more solid record of accomplishment that then makes successive effort easier.

(2) *Council of Ministers.* Given the critical nature of leadership and the critical role of LAFTA in the movement toward a LACM, attention necessarily focuses on LAFTA's Council of Ministers. Created in 1965, the Council was intended to fill the void of no real executive power at ministerial level among member countries able to implement agreements proposed by members.

Initial annual meetings of the Council revealed a basic difference of attitude. For example, as evidenced during the first meeting, some countries clearly favored vigorous action, while others leaned to a cautious approach; however, one tangible accomplishment took the form of a go-ahead for study concerning automatic tariff reductions to replace the customary item-by-item negotiations. Again, the second annual meeting, widely anticipated as likely to indicate the true face of the Council as respects the direction and tempo of integration, proved a disappointment as disagreements ensued between the more developed countries and those less developed—a major disappointment because the disparity between members is great and is not given to speedy change, and so foreshadows continuing difficulty.

Confronted by deeply-imbedded resistances, the Council, additionally, has built-in shortcomings. First, an administrative weakness rests with the gap between preparatory effort at working level and follow-up translation into action plans for members; this weakness suggests the need for more powerful arrangements at central level that can prod execution of development and integration activities at country level. Second, also lacking is an effective central planning organization to examine regional growth; basically, the problem here is two-pronged: (a) LAFTA lacks the machinery that carries sufficient weight with national governments, and (b) national governments continue to think in autarkic terms, inclined to withhold support from integration until assurance of concessions is had from other countries.

Strong central leadership is dependent on strong central administrative machinery. Unfortunately, such leadership, sanctioned by the membership, is difficult to foresee as long as members continue to think in national rather than regional terms. With attitudes in this connection likely to mellow only over time, the prospect may well be that of a long, hard road ahead.

(3) *Planning*. The matter of planning is related, also, to strength of leadership. As intimated earlier, movement towards a LACM can benefit from a coordination of national policies; economic disparities in being, and economic disparities coming into being as a consequence of dissimilar policies, can jeopardize the entire movement (as the will to cooperate is undermined, and as the ability to cooperate is placed under heavy strain). To this end, planning—to foster coordination, and give life to it—assumes a special importance.

An area of central interest in coordination is investment planning. On one score, there are reasons to wish a rational investment pattern. Capital and foreign exchange are in short supply and, so, should be used with care. Efficiency in use is one criterion, but so also are considerations such as avoidance of excessive polarization of industry within the region (the occurrence of which can dull enthusiasm for general cooperation) and the avoidance of overduplication of facilities anywhere. On another score, a coordinated approach to capital procurement holds merit. As suggested earlier, no good purpose is served in a competitive struggle to attract capital from outside the region; nor should one underestimate the good sense of a coordinated appeal in a bid for outside resources (from, say, IDB or the World Bank) when such resources are destined for use along regional lines.

This planning—and resultant coordination along various lines—is not easily attained in a setting such as that of present-day Latin America. Unlike Western Europe, where formation of the EEC required an appeal to, and cooperation from, the leadership of only six countries, the formation of a LACM entails cooperation, and willingness to coordinate, on the part of the leadership of twenty countries—widely differing and, further, already aligned in two differing organizations, CACM and LAFTA. Unlike Western Europe, Latin America is under no great political pressure to pursue integration; in fact, the drives of nationalism comprise a force against integration. Unlike Western Europe, also, Latin America seems not destined to receive external assistance of a magnitude resembling the Marshall Plan. All in all, Latin America faces a strong challenge—one where a dedicated leadership must be assumed a prerequisite of planning in the form that can eventuate in the desired, and required, coordination of effort.

AN ASSESSMENT

Given its goal of development, much thought in Latin America is being directed to the matter of how best to achieve it. A product of this thought—in terms of "a plan" for development—is widespread sentiment in favor of regional economic integration as *the* crucial lever. To this end, current planning is premised heavily on movement toward, and to, a Latin American common market.

The intent, and plan, to link all of Latin America in a common market is ambitious in scope. Certainly the task contemplated is not an easy one. Already many problems, transitional and other, are on hand to beset progress, and others are appearing.

Ostensibly, if the end result is worth going after, the problems enroute can be tackled with purpose in mind and with determination. Among these problems, the central one, unquestionably, involves reconciliation of the fact of "economic disparity" with the expectation of "benefit diffusion."

Chapter 3 / The Status of "Lesser Developed" Countries Within a Latin American Common Market

If integration is to succeed, all the countries must have . . . equal opportunities to profit from the establishment of the common market.

Felipe Herrera, et al.

. . . the problem of reciprocity appears to be the thorniest and most difficult one of all, for it involves a concept that is political, as well as economic, and hence defies measurement.

Miguel S. Wionczek

ECONOMIC integration—the joining together of separate countries to form a more or less unified economic entity—has moved forward dramatically in Latin America during recent years. Long an esteemed ideal, the process of translation into reality found its triggering force in a mounting developmental urge during the post-World War II era. Repeated conferences, dwelling on the imperativeness of development, focused attention increasingly on the potential role of integration. And as familiarity and tactical know-how grew, the scene in due course proved conducive for concrete action. This action came with the close of the 1950s—with the formation of, first, the Central American Common Market (CACM) in 1959 and, second, the Latin American Free Trade Association (LAFTA) in 1960.

The ensuing years witnessed considerable progress as tariffs and related barriers to trade were lowered among members of the two groups of countries. Intra-regional trade rose in volume, significantly altering the split between the intra-regional and extra-regional components of total trade.[1] Moreover, investment showed important reorientation, ostensibly stimulated in given directions by the prospects of enhanced market opportunities within a redefined market framework. Between the two trends—greater intraregional trade and augmented investment of priority types—development received a decided boost. Certain accompanying problems aside, the growing impression was one of integration providing a hopeful means of development inducement and acceleration.

Thus matters stood by 1967. In that year, a monumental further step occurred. The setting was Punta del Este at a meeting convened under auspices of the Organization of American States and attended by, among others, the "heads of state" of all member countries. The issue, once again, was development—only this time with the stress placed squarely on integration as the intermediary. The gist of deliberations was that Latin America should seek to form a single "common market," a Latin American Common Market; that the target date for realization of such full, area-wide integration should be envisioned as no later than 1985, inviting allusion thereafter to the 1970s as "The Decade of Integration." Indeed, adding to an unmistakable aura of deliberateness and determination, the President of the United States, in an on-the-scene address, gave the goal his blessing as he pledged this country's support.[2]

No one expects area-wide integration in Latin America to come about free of all resistance, or even of unbargained-for setbacks. Just as CACM and LAFTA met with problems, so a more expansive movement seems destined not always to enjoy smooth sailing. True, the important matter of who (i.e., what organizational entity, or entities) should spearhead the big drive appears to have been pretty well resolved; LAFTA and CACM are being viewed as providing the base upon which, and via which, to build. But many other matters remain and will need to be dealt with. One of them looms especially large (so large, in fact, that over-all success or failure may well hinge on it): the status to be accorded the "lesser developed" countries of the region.

---

[1] For supporting data, see Table 3, Statistical Appendix.

[2] The "Declaration of the Presidents of America" that followed from the meeting stated as follows: "The President of the U.S. of America, for his part, declares his firm support for this promising Latin American initiative." Excerpts of the "Declaration" appear in the Documents Appendix of this volume; the cited quote appears in Section I. The U.S. President's address, in full, appears in U.S. Department of State *Bulletin* (Washington, D.C., May 8, 1967), pp. 707–12.

NATURE OF THE PROBLEM

Latin America has many cohesive qualities. Despite the number of countries, similarities among them—in culture, in history, in economic attributes—offer a basis for considerable meaningful generalization. Perhaps most basic of all, the countries are linked by the circumstance of underdevelopment. All the countries are underdeveloped, though by no means *equally* so.

Relative to degrees of underdevelopment, we note that per-capita income in Latin America, everywhere vastly lower than in the United States, spans a considerable range: over $500 in Argentina, Uruguay, and Venezuela; under $250 in Bolivia, Haiti, and Paraguay. And while income levels differ, the environments from which income stems also differ widely. The geographic size of Brazil stands in sharp contrast to that of, say, the Central American countries. Similarly, the population of Brazil (over 80 million) dwarfs that of most other countries (under 5 million in roughly a dozen and under 2 million in three). And, of course, some of the countries are well beyond the elementary stages of development, avidly concerned with an emergent industrial complex, while others are less far along, still concerned basically with the traditional raw-materials sector or with the preconditions of infrastructure.[3]

The fact that the countries differ widely in ways such as those mentioned entails interesting implications for development in any event, and especially so when regional integration comprises an integral part of the environmental framework. Within a regional context, competition among countries automatically is accorded greater scope for play—and competition tends, characteristically, to work to the advantage of the "stronger" countries. It is these countries—of best endowment, or simply farthest along developmentally—that stand to benefit most (barring action to the contrary); indeed, some of the benefit that then accrues to them derives, somewhat ironically, from the very participation of countries less well-situated or less far along developmentally.

All the while, the spirit of nationalism is on hand to affect thinking. Basically antagonistic to regionalism, this nationalism is sometimes joined, at times strongly reinforced, by a variety of pressures rooted in narrow self-interest. Given such forces, it is to be expected

---

[3] For basic supporting data on these and related points of diversity, refer to Tables 1 and 2, Statistical Appendix.

that the matter of "split of benefits" should not go unnoted; there is an awareness of how regional integration tends to favor some countries over others, and the response—on one basis or another—frequently is one of outright opposition or of calculated delay.

Thus, three major ingredients, all intertwined, are on the scene. (1) Economic disparities exist among the region's countries. (2) The competition generated under integration favors the stronger countries. (3) Nationalism and self-interest being what they are, integration does not always appear attractive. Given this context, some fundamental questions emerge. Why should a "weaker" country go along with integration? Why, indeed, when it is the growing industrial complexes of countries like Brazil and Argentina that are strengthened—in part through support from the "Bolivias" of the region. If the "weaker" countries need to go along, what reasons can the more-favored countries cite to induce the desired cooperation? What, in fact, do the "Bolivias" of the region stand to gain?

Obviously, there is a problem: the problem of the projected status of the "lesser developed" countries. Unless this matter can be satisfactorily resolved, the cooperation among countries upon which successful integration action hinges can hardly be expected. In terms of our direct interest here, the matter represents *the* basic determinant of the fate of the movement toward a full-scale Latin American Common Market.

Before focusing on what might be done to resolve the foregoing matter in the interests of a LACM, let us survey briefly what preceding integration movements—CACM and LAFTA—have tried to do about it. Perhaps there are lessons in the past that can be brought to bear on future decisions.

EXPERIENCE OF THE PAST

Because the CACM and LAFTA experiences differ somewhat, at least in particular respects, it seems well to consider them separately.

CACM

CACM embraces five small Central American countries (Guatemala through Costa Rica)—all relatively underdeveloped (as compared with, say, Argentina or Brazil), and all rather poorly-situated to promote development unilaterally. Given the uniformity of situation among these countries, there is a basis for considerable cohesion (and, conversely, relatively little basis for a direct conflict of interest).[4] With unilateral action lacking in force, the possibility of greater impact through unison in action readily acquires appeal—the foundation, in fact, of regional integration.

CACM's intended spur to development was seen as linked to reductions in impediments to intra-regional trade, which reductions, in turn, might prompt greater intra-regional trade and the greater investment undertaken in anticipation of greater trade generally. Progress proved gratifying—to an extent that, by the second year of operations, the initial goal of ten years for attainment of free trade within the region could be advanced to just five years. By 1967, some 94 percent of all items listed on tariff schedules stood free of duty and other trade restrictions. Concurrently, the magnitude of intra-regional trade advanced—by over 300 percent (in value) between 1960 and 1965, with the upward movement continuing; alongside of this, intra-regional trade as a proportion of total foreign trade rose—more than tripling between 1960 and 1965 (or from about 6 percent to roughly 20 percent).[5] All the while, investment in new industry was rising significantly, the requisite financing stemming from both indigenous and foreign sources.

Of course, more than just tariff liberalization was responsible for the progress shown. Beneficial impact derived also from (1) the movement to a common external tariff, (2) the introduction of a zonal payments system, and (3) the decision to support special "integration industries." Relative to (1), the goal, by 1970, of uniform duties on imports originating outside the region was substantially attained by 1967, at which time imports so treated exceeded 80 percent. A co-effect of encouragement of intra-regional trade at the expense of imports of extra-regional origin was the further buttressing of incentives for investment in new industry within the region.

Relative to (2), new arrangements were instituted to assist the clearance and settlement of trade balances among countries of the region.[6] Supplementary arrangements were concerned with the harmonization of monetary and credit policies among countries of the

---

[4] See Tables 1 and 2, Statistical Appendix.

[5] Summary trade data for CACM appear in Table 13, Statistical Appendix.

[6] Introduced in 1961, the Central American Clearing House was, by 1965, handling over 90 percent of all transactions between members. Creation of a Central American Peso further facilitated the clearance process; used in the settlement of intra-regional balances, its effect was to lessen the need to draw down scarce external reserves.

region, preparatory to eventual movement to full monetary union.[7]

Relative to (3), the problem of individual countries being too small to sustain many types of industry was countered with the idea of "integration industries": the selection for establishment within the region of specific industries, each to enjoy a monopoly-like status,[8] and each placed geographically, per plan, so as to give every country some industry. Success for such industries was regarded likely by virtue of (a) free access to a unified five-country market area, (b) sheltered from external competition by the presence of a common external tariff. Despite a slow start, projected action in this vein pointed to a more substantive future.

LAFTA

A crucial factor in the success generally ascribed to CACM was the extent of harmony among its members, a harmony helped by high similarity of situation among them. A like environment was never the case for LAFTA. There it was a matter of big countries alongside small countries; of relatively far-advanced countries alongside countries still quite underdeveloped; of Brazil, Argentina, etc., alongside Paraguay and Ecuador.[9]

That the successful merger of countries so diverse would require special provisions was recognized in LAFTA from the outset. In most basic terms, member countries were classed in three categories in accordance with similarities of developmental status: (1) the most developed countries (Argentina, Brazil, and Mexico), (2) countries in an "insufficient market" state (Colombia, Chile, Peru, Uruguay,[10] and Venezuela[11]), and (3) the relatively less developed countries

---

[7] The Central American Monetary Union, introduced in 1964, was expected eventually to absorb the Clearing House.

[8] Because monopoly conditions readily invite abuse, certain control tactics—all indirect—were outlined.

[9] Refer again to Tables 1 and 2, Statistical Appendix.

[10] LAFTA's Council of Ministers, during its 1967 sessions, reclassified Uruguay as "lesser developed" for the period up to 1972.

[11] Though provided for by LAFTA as indicated, Venezuela continued to occupy an "intermediate" status, short of full-fledged membership, as late as 1968. Similarly, Bolivia, classed by LAFTA as a relatively less developed country, had not as yet, by that year, moved beyond introductory phases in the acquisition of membership.

(Bolivia, Ecuador, and Paraguay[12]).[13] Supplementary to this, forms of special treatment for "weaker" countries were cited, covering (1) the implementation of reductions in tariffs and other trade restrictions, (2) the amelioration of balance-of-payments difficulties, and (3) the introduction or expansion of specific productive activities.[14] Thereafter, as LAFTA has pushed forward, each resolution of major substance has continued to reflect a concern for those countries confronted with inhibiting circumstances.

The basic rationale of LAFTA, as in the case of CACM, was that of reductions in tariffs and other barriers to trade between member countries in the interests of greater intra-regional trade and, along with it, greater investment, output, etc. The intent was that of progressive reductions in barriers to intra-regional trade, resulting in "free trade" within the region[15] by the end of twelve years.[16] Concurrently, in the hope of smoothing the path of trade liberalization, the intent was for a closer coordination among countries of planning effort[17] and of actions generally.

Although the over-all intent unmistakably was for swift trade liberalization, circumstances and situations were such as to seem to warrant the retention of a number of important "loopholes." Always the alternatives posed for LAFTA were (a) to try to compel a similar response by every member, whatever its status, and thereby perhaps give some member no choice but non-participation, or (b) to try to provide a livable avenue for the member with a "special" problem and thereby assist it in participation to the best of its capacity. Given

---

12 Relative to non-LAFTA portions of Latin America, probably rating categorization under (3) also are the CACM countries, along with the island countries of the Caribbean plus Panama.

13 Resolution 71-III (of the Contracting Parties of LAFTA) expressed the intent of "a just distribution of the benefits . . . [of integration]" for countries having "insufficient markets" or being "less developed."

14 Under Article 32 (of the Treaty of Montevideo, which established LAFTA).

15 While CACM aimed for a "common market" (free trade within the region, but with a common external tariff relative to imports of extra-regional origin), LAFTA was intended to yield a "free trade area"—free trade within the region, but with each member country remaining free to fix its own tariff levels on imports of extra-regional origin. After the Punta del Este meeting (April 1967), however, LAFTA's goal was advanced from simple free trade to that of a full-fledged common market—with a LACM envisaged as the product of a merging of CACM and LAFTA.

16 By 1973.

17 Expressed, if not enforced.

the alternatives, LAFTA leaned to (b). Thus, relative to items of intra-regional trade on the so-called National List (on which duty reductions of no less than 8 percent per year were contemplated, all such reductions normally generalized thereafter via most-favored-nation treatment), member countries retained the discretionary right under an "escape clause" provision to withdraw concessions[18] in the event of balance-of-payments difficulties[19] or of serious threat to output vital to national well-being;[20] or, under circumstances of pressure, remained eligible to request approval for release from even the commitment to enter into an annual round of reductions.[21] Further, relative to items on the Common List (to which 25 percent of all items in intra-regional trade were to be added every three years, resulting in virtually all such items being embraced by target-year 1973), disproportionately heavy adjustment pressure expected to fall upon some members in the course of compliance with planned duty reductions was cited as justification for a slower pace in reductions in particular instances, such as in the case of certain agricultural products of dominant importance to the lesser developed countries.

In another respect, relative to "complementation agreements" (which aim at immediate free trade between two or more countries in a specified product or group of products, chiefly in the industrial sector), little or no success has been had in helping the lesser developed countries. The early expectation that such agreements would help to attract major industrial investment even to small otherwise-poorly-situated countries (since resultant output, however limited its market at home, then stood free of barriers in its movement to the partner countries, where the major market presumably lay) simply has not proven out in practice. In fact, sentiment in the lesser developed countries has turned critical on grounds that complementation agreements may, as they have been used, actually contribute to a further polarization of industry in the already more advanced areas.[22]

---

[18] From the National List.

[19] In the absence of other balance-of-payments support (say, an IMF-type of support), the alternatives open to a country quickly reduce to (a) withdrawal from a concession or (b) outright non-participation in LAFTA.

[20] Countries invoking the escape clause (relative to a limited number of products) have included Chile, Colombia, and Uruguay.

[21] A prerogative exercised by, for example, Ecuador and Paraguay.

[22] Four major complementation agreements had been concluded by 1966: statistical machines (Argentina, Brazil, Chile, and Uruguay); electronic tubes (Argentina, Brazil, Mexico, and Uruguay); household electrical appliances (Brazil

Similarly, the principle of "margin of preference," introduced with the lesser developed countries in mind,[23] has not proven a success in its translation into practice. The intent, of course, was to assure the lesser developed countries of favored treatment (i.e., a margin of preference) in the scheduling of tariff reductions in the hope of achieving (a) greater substitution, within these countries, of domestic output for customary imports, and (b) improved access externally (in the markets of better-situated countries in LAFTA) for domestic output. Yet, little was accomplished in this direction—though "pro" sentiment in the lesser developed countries, always strong, proved a factor in evoking renewed consideration of the matter more recently.[24]

Data are on hand, to be sure, to shed light on the extent of success, overall, in expanding intra-regional trade. Intra-regional trade has been rising within the LAFTA area (though not as dramatically as within CACM)—in index terms, intra-regional trade rose from 100 to 222 between 1961 and 1966, while extra-regional trade rose from 100 to 126; intra-regional trade as a proportion of total foreign trade roughly doubled (from about 6 percent to almost 11 percent).[25] A major portion of the increase unquestionably should be ascribed to tariff-cutting, though, as in the case of CACM, improvements in payments arrangements,[26] etc., surely also contributed in this direction.

In short, trade liberalization, reinforced with other actions, resulted in the significantly greater intra-regional trade that had been sought in the interests of developmental promotion. However, as intra-regional trade increased overall, gains at the individual-country level did not necessarily accrue as intended or expected. Actually, the distribution-by-country of intra-regional trade changed little during the period; the more developed countries (especially Argentina and Bra-

---

and Uruguay); and electronic and electrical communications equipment (Brazil and Uruguay). Thereafter, three more agreements were concluded, but these have been put in force only partially, or not at all. For a full list, plus further details, see Table 8, Statistical Appendix.

[23] Resolution 53-II (of the Contracting Parties of LAFTA).

[24] By LAFTA's Council of Ministers at its 1967 meeting, where a proposal for a three-category regimen of preferential margins was advanced.

[25] Refer again to Table 3, Statistical Appendix.

[26] LAFTA is evolving a zonal payments system, based on a network of bilateral agreements between central banks. Initiated only in 1966, early experience indicates multilateralized compensation arrangements embracing something over 30 percent of potentially coverable transactions.

zil) continue to dominate intra-regional trade, while the shares of lesser developed countries remain small and have even decreased for some (e.g., Ecuador and Paraguay).

CURRENT STATUS AND FUTURE PROSPECTS

As the foregoing reveals, LAFTA has encountered problems far more formidable than has CACM. This has been the case not so much because of any difference in diligence of effort, but more directly because of a difference of environment. Unlike CACM, comprised of countries of roughly similar status, LAFTA has had to work with countries of assorted status. Indeed, the contrast in the two experiences has provided a lesson: diversity invites disunity—which situation, unless countered, impairs the very basis for successful integration.

The problems of LAFTA within an eleven-country context are a matter of record. Looking ahead, it seems only reasonable to expect similar problems, on a grander scale, within the context of all of Latin America as the movement to a full LACM proceeds. The big problem, rooted in diversity, does not, of course, rest fundamentally with the more advanced countries; these countries are moving ahead, and stand to move ahead even faster as the benefits of integration accrue. The problem rests, rather, with the lesser developed countries. There can be no true regional integration without these countries; yet, cooperation on their part presumes "adequate" benefits for them as well as for the more advanced countries.

Thus, the thesis here is that the leaders of integration, as they push to hasten the shift to a LACM, should be concerned—probably even more concerned than in the past—with the status of the lesser developed countries. In this connection, four areas of potential activity seem especially to merit attention: (1) subregional integration, (2) sector integration, (3) intra-regional financing, and (4) the exercise of leadership (apropos the role of the Council of Ministers of LAFTA).

SUBREGIONAL INTEGRATION

The rationale for subregional integration is simple: to ease the transition to region-wide integration, integration can advantageously be pursued first within smaller blocs (within subregions, each fairly homogeneous and, hence, fairly conducive to progress), leaving until later—to a time when substantial headway has been made at subregional levels—the final drive to all-out amalgamation. Actually, the

CACM area comprises such a subregion;[27] and, more recently, a further subregional movement of note has taken hold: the so-called Andean Group, linking Bolivia, Chile, Colombia, Ecuador, Peru, and Venezuela.[28]

To illustrate with the Andean Group, the participating countries seemed to have much in common that might facilitate immediate progress. All were "lesser developed"—relative to, say, Argentina and Brazil. If within the same framework as the more advanced countries, competitive forces threatened to retard development within them; but if joined together in an arrangement somewhat apart from the more advanced countries, prospects seemed improved for autonomous development (involving, say, investment in the industrial sector) somewhere within their confines. Accordingly, steps were taken to initiate a working arrangement that might result in, first, greater coordination in the over-all policies affecting development and, second, some amount of tangible action yielding immediate development. As evidence of work during several official meetings, the Andean Group has proven instrumental in (a) the formulation of agreements for the joint development of the petro-chemical and machinery industries and for the integration of the automobile industry, (b) the acceptance of a schedule of accelerated tariff reductions within the subregion, (c) the establishment of a pattern for a common external tariff, and (d) the creation of a mechanism intended to ease the settlement of trade accounts among the participants.[29]

---

27 The procedure of "subregional agreements" as a transitional tactic in integration first gained recognition within LAFTA during a 1964 meeting in Bogota. Though CACM had earlier origins, its identification as a subregion-in-fact came only with the cited meeting.

28 The Andean Subregional Group, in process of formation over several years, was joined by its newest member, Bolivia, during 1967. Formed in anticipation of compliance within the framework of LAFTA's over-all rules, the Andean Group was not accorded full legal standing under LAFTA until 1969; long pending was the requisite action by LAFTA in agreeing on the compatibility of the Andean Group's statutes with the Treaty of Montevideo. While thus long remaining short of formal endorsement under LAFTA, the Andean Group nonetheless proceeded with the formation of organizational sub-structures of its own. Most important, the Andean Development Corporation (ADC) was introduced; patterned along lines of the Chilean Development Corporation, the role envisaged for ADC related to the financing of preinvestment and investment needs within the area, in essence providing the member countries with their counterpart of the CACM area's Central American Bank for Economic Integration.

29 The arrangements under (d), standing beyond the ADC "regional bank" concept, bear strong similarities to the CACM area's "Cámara de Compensación Centro Americana."

Given the immensity of the task involved in moving to a LACM, the merits of subregional integration as an intermediary step would appear to warrant careful consideration. In all this, the Andean Group, a major movement of considerable area-coverage, would seem a "model" worth watching (capable of providing important insights alongside lessons already on hand via the CACM "subregional" arrangement). Possibilities clearly exist for further subregions, as well as for revised combinations of countries within subregions—even as, with experience, more activities come to be accepted as properly within the scope of whatever subregions are on the scene.

SECTOR INTEGRATION

Just as the impediment inherent in diversity-among-countries stands to be breached when integration effort is applied somewhat selectively in terms of a smaller area (subregional integration), so a sectoral approach (sector integration)—under which integration is aimed not at all products at once or at random, but at one product or at one group of products at a time—stands to ease the pangs of the integration process. However difficult across-the-board integration may be (and difficulties aplenty are usual), some integration, involving only some lines of activity, may nevertheless prove an immediate possibility—and, hence, merit serious consideration.

Little has occurred thus far in Latin America in the realm of sector integration. True, LAFTA has given attention to three important sectors: iron and steel, petro-chemicals, and paper and cellulose; however, only the first two have appeared even likely for area-wide treatment. Nor has much been accomplished with the closely-related procedure of complementation agreements (under which two or more countries can establish immediate free trade in covered items, sheltering them from outside competition with a common external tariff). In fact, sentiment in the lesser developed countries has turned somewhat critical of the sectoral approach, whatever its form. All too often the impression has been that intra-regional sector linkages work in favor of the stronger producers, generally situated in the more advanced countries rather than in the lesser developed countries.

Yet, the technique(s) would seem to hold potential for the lesser developed countries, and, therefore, merit further consideration as to possible successful application. Certain circumstances are imaginable under which a lesser developed country might well carve out a role: (1) multi-product producers might find advantages in dispersing some portion of their production capacity; (2) components of a product might be produced in quite a number of locales, in anticipation of shipment to a major locale for final assembly; and (3) dissimilar phases of production in a multi-stage production process might be carried out in widely-separated locales, with final assembly or processing centered in some major locale.

INTRA-REGIONAL FINANCING

Many associate heavy financial outlay with a program of integration: not only are projects costly in the aggregate, but the seriousness of effort itself depends on the adequacy of backing. Others, in fundamental agreement as to probable costliness, go on, however, to contend that financing poses no immediate constraint; sufficient financing to service current activity is available, they suggest, or can be made available through existing arrangements—through, say, the Inter-American Development Bank (IDB) or like institutions.

Yet, even if financing seems adequate in some over-all sense, can it be regarded as adequate also in terms of the needs of the relatively less developed countries? Is it not possible that available financing will, in the absence of special arrangements to the contrary, simply come to be applied very largely in the countries already more developed? If such is a strong likelihood, is there not then a case for evolving supplementary procedures that can give the lesser developed countries a better prospect for new production facilities? Not only is there reason to believe that something further along these lines is in order to place the lesser developed countries more nearly on a par with better-situated countries,[30] but a body of thought already exists as to the form this support might take.

One approach, perhaps best thought of in terms of initial application solely within the LAFTA area (where diversity among countries

30 The reasoning ordinarily associated draws upon factual material such as the following: the IDB, while committed in principle to favorable treatment of lesser developed countries, nevertheless is responsible primarily to *all* of Latin America; the ADC is committed to service the Andean Group, not lesser developed countries, per se; the Central American Bank for Economic Integration is committed to service the CACM area, not lesser developed countries, per se. In sum, no one of the major prevailing institutions bears an all-out responsibility toward, expressly, the lesser developed countries.

is currently felt most keenly), is to establish a special "integration fund" on behalf of development in the lesser developed countries. Contributions could come from all members—computed, say, as a small percentage of current GNP. Eligibility for financing—on a loan basis—could extend to projects in lesser developed countries, and to those multi-country projects involving directly one or more of the lesser developed countries. Administration could be by the IDB, already widely referred to as the "Bank for Integration."[31]

Ostensibly, two main advantages could derive from an arrangement of the suggested type. First, lesser developed countries could reasonably envisage enhanced developmental potential for themselves, and, hence, could afford to feel greater enthusiasm in their over-all participation. Second, all countries would stand to be drawn together more closely, thereby strengthening the basic integration spirit.

INTEGRATION'S LEADERSHIP

What will happen with integration depends, in important measure, on how responsibility is exercised in the initiation and implementation of action. With LAFTA a critical component within the total context, attention of necessity is directed to its Council of Ministers. There, however, good cause may exist for some second thoughts.

Weak initially because of no provision for executive power at the ministerial level, LAFTA was subsequently provided with leadership in the form of a Council of Ministers. In practice, the Council has been composed mainly of Ministers of Foreign Relations, not of representatives from more-directly-concerned, or more-powerfully-situated, economic ministries—e.g., Ministers of Industry or Commerce—as true in the case of CACM's counterpart. The major problems of integration have been, and remain, economic, not diplomatic

[31] While the IDB can (and does) service multi-country projects of the type cited (encompassing lesser developed countries or these countries *and* more advanced countries), the suggested "integration fund" would be "self-financed" —*by* Latin America, *for* the lesser developed countries of Latin America (or, in the case of LAFTA, *by* LAFTA countries, *for* the lesser developed countries within LAFTA)—unlike the IDB procedure, which extends beyond Latin America in its reliance on "foreign" participation (e.g., cooperating funds of United States, and other-country, origin). In sum, the suggested "integration fund" involves something beyond what currently prevails.

—thereby suggesting that a changed composition, to assure a different type of talent and outlook, is in order.

Not only is there question as to the Council's representation, but also as to its administrative procedures in the handling of work. Unlike CACM, which aims at all but final agreement on agenda items prior to the convening of a formal meeting, LAFTA, in its practices to date, is prone to see a considerable amount of early-stage work come before the formal meeting itself. Preferable, seemingly, would be a greater thrashing out of preparatory matters at the "working level," sparing the Council of excessive detail and possible diversionary debate when it does convene.

THE BIGGER PICTURE

Admittedly, more can be done in Latin America to prod integration—which, if to prove successful, has to assure all countries, including the lesser developed countries, of benefits. Yet, not everything that is germane to the success of integration lies within Latin America's power. What Latin America can do is much affected by the greater environment—by what happens *outside* the region, as well as within. Many elements are involved: the extent of global well-being, economically and politically; the nature of the rules that govern international trade; the status of capital flows, public and private. If, however, this greater environment is reasonably favorable, Latin America seemingly has every reason to expect decided gains from her own efforts in perfecting the course of integration.

Chapter 4 / The Latin American Common Market: Prospects and Implications

The task at hand is not an easy one, but it is the only one possible.

Eduardo Frei

The Latin American quest . . . is of much more than local significance: its lessons are of deep significance for the political economy of the underdeveloped world as a whole.

Sidney Dell

In swift succession, Latin America has taken a series of steps intended, in the end, to yield a region-wide common market. These steps, in sequence, have carried Latin America from a situation a decade ago when the common market was but an idea, through an intermediary stage during which the CACM and LAFTA organizations were introduced and pushed forward, and on to a more recent stage of direct concern with the ultimate goal of a fully "Latin American" common market. It was in Punta del Este during 1967 that the "heads of state" of the hemisphere approved the "Declaration of the Presidents of America"—formally endorsing a movement toward, and to, a Latin American Common Market (LACM), to be substantially attained by no later than 1985.

Today, in the wake of the historic events of 1967, attention is on arranging the necessary groundwork, on devising methods of countering known roadblocks, and on initiating the requisite actions of implementation. Much lies between the present and a definitive outcome, but a number of major implications logically impinge in any event. It is these implications that provide the primary focus for this chapter—commentary extending, in fact, to (a) the policy posture *now* appropriate for the United States in the light of Latin America's actions, and (b) the *probable* (as distinct from possible) direction of Latin America's future.

IMPLICATIONS

Admittedly, movement toward a full common market—intended to yield (a) a single market area, (b) sheltered, as an entity, against outside competition—envisages environmental change of major scope. Turning to implications that expectedly attend such change, a creditable starting point is the structure of production and trade.

PRODUCTION AND TRADE

For Latin America, the basic rationale for a common market is "promotion of development." The reasoning is simple: potential access to a wider (and protected) market area enhances trade prospects for output arising anywhere within the region, thereby (a) underwriting this output (particularly manufacturing output, highly dependent on economies of scale) and, even more basic, (b) stimulating the investment itself that is presumed to give rise to the end-output and trade. In essence, a wider market area is desired not so much for reasons of trade expansion pursuant to the already-existing pattern of production (regarded as deficient anyway) as for reasons of inducing added investment to create new productive capacity, leading to an altered pattern of production (and, through such structural change, inviting greater employment and income—the very substance of development). Contrasted with Western Europe, where a common market is thought of in terms of added material benefits resulting from a better allocation of effort within the context of a rather well-defined production order already on hand, the Latin American premise is that a common market provides a means via which to shift from an inadequate production order of long-standing to a new and preferred production order. The shift is envisaged as occurring through an acceleration particularly of industrial development to form an important adjunct to all else—an acceleration process dependent on an adequate trade outlet for output, thereby contributing to an adequate motivation for the investment that yields this output.

Given the foregoing observations, we are able to deduce that *if* success follows from effort, not only will Latin America derive developmental benefit, but, as a companion feature, will find its production and trade assuming both a different level and a different pattern. And if Latin America's production-and-trade configuration is so altered, it follows, of necessity, that adjustment is entailed for trading partners situated elsewhere; certainly, the foreign trade of the developed countries beyond Latin America stands thereby to be affected, both in composition and volume.

We have said "if success follows." But *will* it follow? On this score, we can cite here, preliminarily, good reasons as to why it *can* follow—and why, thus, the adjustments of which we speak become substantive. Among these reasons, two appear to merit emphasis: the sheer strength of the common market technique as a developmental lever, and, related to this, the direct implications for foreign investment inherent in a common market approach. Let us turn to these.

(1) *Developmental lever.* The movement in Latin America to a full common market may well be (indeed, probably *is*) the "number one" developmental lever that the region has at its disposal. In direct comparison with anything else one might reasonably cite, the developmental impact-potential of a common market movement is simply enormous; there is nothing "halfway" about such a movement seriously pursued, since it offers a way to get at structural change in a forthright and essentially forceful manner.

(2) *A lure to foreign investment.* A common market movement offers inducement-potential for investment—not only investment of indigenous origin (as previously explained), but also investment of foreign origin (thereby reinforcing the lever aspect mentioned above). Producers in developed-country locales external to the region, accustomed to servicing the Latin American market(s) with output from abroad, are given special reason to contemplate investment (production) within Latin America because of (a) the attraction added by the possibility of unencumbered product movement within the region, alongside (b) the new deterrent, in the form of a uniform tariff around the region, confronting an attempt at continued product entry from abroad. Indeed, if the "UNCTAD idea" (of preferential tariff treatment by developed countries for potential inflows of manufactured goods from underdeveloped countries, alongside continued admissibility of tariff protection by under-

developed countries against inflows of competitive manufactured goods from developed countries) should be activated as an accompaniment of the common market movement, we can foresee yet another inducement factor for foreign investment in Latin America (and for other as-yet underdeveloped locales).[1] Then, investment in Latin America for production there might occur on the assumption of end-output access to the markets of both (a) the Latin American region and (b) the developed-country regions beyond it.

(3) *Latin America and beyond.* As we thus suggest, the common market movement carries the implication of trade impact on Latin America and on Latin America's trading partners. We need, however, to go farther and suggest that this impact stands to magnify over time; at least, the probability is definitely in this direction if other underdeveloped regions, beyond Latin America, *also* proceed with common market plans. As matters stand, Latin America—perhaps most advanced, in general, among the major underdeveloped regions—is "out in front" in the realm of common market involvement. But, as it is with pioneering, the Latin American involvement may merely foreshadow what others will seek to emulate at some point, viewing prior actions and experiences as "the model." Should these other regions actually so proceed (as well they might if Latin America's record reveals sufficient promise), then the impact, *globally,* on trade levels and patterns can likely prove very considerable.

Even today, one notes that the common market idea is being "tossed around" in some other quarters of the underdeveloped world —in parts of Asia and Africa. Given this general interest and the possibilities thereby opened, it seems not amiss to speculate about a future world of a limited number of trading blocs, perhaps linked under circumstances of special trading arrangements.

INTERNATIONAL ARRANGEMENTS

Turning to another facet, certain international arrangements, long established and even hallowed, are threatened under pressure from the common market. Examples include the multilateralist philosophy and GATT, and the "aid framework."

[1] Excerpts from the "Final Report" growing out of the UNCTAD I conference appear in the Documents Appendix. Also appearing there is an assessment of the "UNCTAD movement."

(1) *Multilateralism and GATT.*[2] A common market presupposes the presence of a consciously-contrived amalgamation of a number of countries into a single regional economic bloc. The end result—indeed, the movement toward it—stands in contrast to the multi-countried, unilaterally-acting community of nations assumed as a working condition under the philosophy of multilateralism. Put bluntly, the common market movement in Latin America is in conflict with the ideal of multilateralism.

While the foregoing might be cited as true also of Western Europe and the EEC, there is, nonetheless, a difference; Latin America involves twenty countries, not just six as initially under the EEC—and, in addition, the Latin American experience *could* prove a forerunner among the underdeveloped regions, as we have conjectured, and thereby bring the foreseeable global coverage up to half or more of all countries. Indeed, already on hand to accentuate the whole anti-multilateralist trend, in Latin America and also beyond, are other powerful forces. To be specific, the "UNCTAD idea," widely subscribed to in Latin America (and in other underdeveloped regions) in great part *because* of its discriminatory features that clearly run counter to multilateral precepts, dovetails beautifully with the developmental goal envisaged under the common market movement, actually reinforcing it. Further, the GATT organization, continuing in its formal role as foremost espouser and guardian of multilateralist principles as a guide to practice, is currently under heavy fire in select quarters of Latin America, with mass rejection (by possibly all Latin American members from among a global complement of but roughly sixty countries) periodically threatened.

The gist is that the ingredients are on hand, within and because of the common market movement, to initiate the demise of multilateralism as a guiding principle and of GATT as a working instrumentality. The implications of such an eventuality clearly are enormous, not only for regional and global trade, but also for the rules that surround the conduct of this trade and of economic activity generally.

(2) *The "aid framework."* The traditional concept of foreign aid is that of a residual derived from external donors in order to offset insufficiencies in the composite of ordinary trade and investment—whatever residual so derived, further, being funneled inwards to, and

[2] A statement on GATT principles, in the form of excerpts from the GATT charter, appears in the Documents Appendix.

on behalf of, single-country beneficiaries. Under a common market or a movement to such, if taken at face value, all this quite obviously merits recasting. On a first score, foreign aid along traditional lines of special inflow then enters a regional context, and thus appropriately deserves being approached on a multi-country, not a single-country, programming basis. Clearly, changes in aid forms are called for—*if* traditional aid is to continue and is to prove truly pertinent. Significantly, however, traditional aid—in *any* form—is itself deserving of reappraisal, given the new frame of reference.

Traditional aid stands to undergo de-emphasis with advancement of the common market movement—not that such aid then no longer possesses potential value, but because new and powerful ways are brought into play for garnering the equivalent. Specifically, a common market movement (especially if matched with action also on an "UNCTAD idea") can breathe new life into the old aim of self-help. The attack then is in terms of "changing the rules" in a manner that improves the prospects for the subject countries to "earn their own way." Instead of aid as something material specially introduced because of insufficiencies in trade and investment, the thought is to enhance trade to the point that trade plus induced investment make much less central the need for a special aid influx.

In substance, thus, emphasis shifts from traditional aid to "changing the rules" in order to give new meaning to self-help. In place of the old-line slogan of "Trade, Investment, *and* Aid," or even that of "Trade, *not* Aid," the new slogan characterizing matters becomes "Trade *is* Aid."

ACADEMIC STUDY

It follows, too, that the common market movement has implications for academic study. Academicians like to think of themselves as generating the ideas that then provide a basis for "real world" action. In the present instance, with the common market movement *a fact,* we find, however, the strange circumstance of havoc having been dealt big chunks of established subject matter and, alongside it, of academicians left behind to shore up their materials to fit the new "real world" situation. We can see this both in (a) the content of Economic Development and in (b) the relationships of this subject to companion disciplines.

(1) *The subject of Economic Development.* In theory and practice, economic development, as traditionally represented and presented, has its concern with how to overcome certain forces within a given country so as to turn a vicious circle into an upward surge; the single-country orientation is basic, conditioning how a vicious circle is to be attacked and how an upward surge is to be sought. When a common market is contemplated or on hand, in contrast, thinking and action no longer need to be—entirely or even largely—single-country oriented; the context then is multi-country, actually and deliberately. In essence, the environment is different; and *because* the environment is different, there is a new latitude for ideas and applications—a latitude that, in fact, justifies ideas and applications beyond those pertinent to a single-country orientation.

To illustrate the distinction, self-help for development can mean something very different within a multi-country context than within a single-country context. Within a single-country context, self-help ordinarily is treated in terms of looking *inwards* relative to the generation of developmental ingredients and their placement. Within a multi-country context, in contrast, self-help can seek expression, additionally, through resort to new "gimmicks"—new lines of attack on the development problem. Indeed, the very presence of a new multi-country arrangement, altering the status of members vis-a-vis one another and of all vis-a-vis the rest of the world, represents a gimmick—one from which, in turn, other gimmicks can flow. The development approach then needs not be focused exclusively, or even heavily, inwards; it can be focused *outwards*—toward external relations and relationships. Perhaps the tactic of a simple "change in the rules" as to how an economy is to fit into the regional or global structure can provide a developmental impetus that far surpasses anything potentially possible under traditional single-country rules and procedures. It is this possibility, indeed, that prompts the comment as to the "legal avenue" (of rules change) conceivably offering more pro-developmental potential than any readily imaginable amount of scheming and skimping by a single country within strictly its own confines.

What is at issue is the "rules of the game." Under economic development, as traditionally represented and presented, each country looks unto itself, assuming as a given the rules that stand between it and others. Once a common market is introduced, economic development has another variable to contend with (or play with!): individual countries are party to a movement under which the rules that stand between them, and between them and others, not only are (a) *open to change,* but (b) changeable, to a point, *at their discretion.*

The significance of the foregoing is that the economics profession has produced literally tons of material about the "theory and practice" of development under the first frame of reference, but to this day there is remarkably little around that is premised on a common market being a "number one" gimmick of development. The evidence is clear; one needs only to check the substance of the array of development texts on hand and currently emerging.

If there is ground for criticism of our stock of literature as we now know it, there is implicit in the situation, also, an opportunity. There is need for development economists to turn their talents to a "development economics" that has direct relevance within the new environment of which we speak; that, at the very least, can provide a "helping hand" to those who are in a position to shape, in one way or another, the new environment. Illustrative of the type of work that merits attention, let us refer to three specifics—tying each to the "need for economic advice" in Latin America as its common market movement proceeds.

First, realization by Latin America of its common market ambitions entails turning that region into a single market area. The same is true of any major region that proceeds likewise, so that a spreading of the common market idea can give us, in the end, a world of a relatively few large market areas, each reasonably unified within but each also separated fairly sharply from the others. This is a world far different than that presumed by classical economics (as embodied in the so-called "pure theory" of international trade that, in turn, is today being freely drawn upon by many development economists). In fact, the economics that befits this new world is scarcely touched upon today—or, insofar as presented, is certainly not regarded as the standard economics. Minimally, further work merits being done to assure the generalized framework that, as a norm, might be drawn upon for reasonably reliable policy guidance in coping with questions such as: What is comparative advantage? What investments, and where, are justified? What trading relationships should be fostered, and how?

Second, the planning literature of today is single-country oriented; to the extent that multi-country planning (regional planning) enters the usual text, it is presented somewhat as an afterthought, a section added after the "main" story has been told. If multi-country effort holds the implications for development that we have pictured, then multi-country (regional) planning appears much in order; the supporting literature, for purposes of understanding and guidance, should be on hand. Many questions exist to which answers are needed: Should each country in a common market grouping, such as Latin America's, plan independently and then attempt to coordinate? If so, how is coordination to be handled? If investment for infrastructure and in projects can be coordinated, how about coordination relative to such more general propositions as monetary policy and fiscal policy?

Third, circumstances under the common market movement in Latin America suggest a need to review the status of "foreign aid." According to some recent commentary, the era of "traditional aid" (grant or loan) is ending anyway, though ostensibly for reasons other than the circumstance of a common market movement. Whether ending or not, the point here is another one: that the altered environment under a common market movement deserves recognition when the aid matter is under consideration. Traditional aid, if to continue at all, merits a regional programming treatment when the environment it enters is highlighted by a multi-country approach to development. More important still, traditional aid, however programmed, may simply have lost claim to central status in the shift to a multi-country approach to development; as suggested earlier, the truly relevant relationship under a common market is expressed in the slogan "Trade *is* Aid."

(2) *Tie to International Business.* Given a common market movement, a foremost developmental lever is that of inducement for investment (in the wake of upgraded trade prospects). This investment can be either indigenous, using capital from within the region, or external, involving capital from outside the region. To the extent that external investment enters (which could prove substantial), developmental promotion occurs along lines of activity quite central to a companion discipline of rapidly rising interest: International Business.

With emphasis on the common market technique in development, the subject-matter content of Economic Development is brought closer to some of the substantive aspects (e.g., investment and enterprise in an international setting) of International Business; and, conversely, International Business is thereby provided with a highly relevant claim to involvement in the matter of development. In effect, the disciplines of International Business and Economic Development *share* a considerable span of similar ground—a fact driven home by the role of external investment (foreign enterprise) in the developmental process under the environment of a common market movement.

Actually, while the content of Economic Development is undergoing change (and is under pressure to undergo further change), so, also, the content of International Business is coming to reflect a considerable concern about development (and is under pressure to reflect such concern even more). Through all this (and of special interest to academicians), the two disciplines, simply by addressing themselves to ongoing world trends, appear *drawn to* a position of strong mutual reinforcement.

THE U.S. POSTURE

Beyond the foregoing, there are other implications that follow from a Latin American common market movement. Among them, one particularly merits our attention: the matter of the "appropriate" official policy response of the United States to what is occurring, or projected, in Latin America. In this connection, a proposal is here advanced for consideration.

A PROPOSAL

During the "heads of state" meeting in Punta del Este in 1967, the United States officially placed itself on record as favoring the formation of a LACM. Indeed, not only did the United States, along with other OAS countries, formally subscribe to the "Declaration of the Presidents of America," but the then United States President, in an address during a personal appearance, stated in so many words that this country felt an obligation in terms of both moral and other support.[3] Thus, the United States came through with a position *and* an associated "promise"—but, after the passage of nearly two years, there was no "follow up" with the concrete forms of reinforcement supposedly implied earlier.

Against this background, we subscribe to the view that the United States should *now* move beyond "moral support" and begin to come

---

[3] See again the earlier reference to the Presidential statement appearing in Chapter 3 (fn. 2).

through with "concrete forms of reinforcement"—doing so because (a) Latin America needs the reinforcement, lest otherwise the common market movement falters, and because (b) the United States' own self-interest, relative to Latin America, dictates such reinforcement. In line with this view, the pertinent question is that of *what,* precisely, the United States should do.

With a new Administration in Washington,[4] ready to give numerous things a "second look," the current juncture is perhaps an opportune time to "take stock" of the United States-Latin American relationship. As a prior condition to virtually any "second look," however, certain factors doubtless deserve recognition, if not acceptance. The new Administration is quite budget conscious—which means that any course entailing high cost (in direct governmental outlay) appears not overly welcome. Conversely, the new Administration appears rather receptive to "inducement mechanisms"—to modes of approach that rely on incentives for achieving desired actions and results, thereby obviating the demand for costly direct governmental outlay.

Given the foregoing governmental "climate" in the United States, and given that this country does want a favorable working relationship with Latin America (with Latin America for sure, because of sharing a Western Hemisphere location), we are able to present the outlines of a particular proposal. Succinctly, the United States should do the following:

(1) It should reiterate support, moral and other, for Latin America's common market movement.

(2) *Concurrently* with this, it should announce that, on its part, it is willing to enter into discussions, *now,* to arrange preferential tariff treatment for manufactured-goods output from Latin America.

In this way, the United States would be unveiling a new program toward Latin America, one that (a) builds on the past, (b) can prod economic activity in Latin America, (c) costs the United States literally nothing in direct governmental outlay, and, yet, (d) offers diplomatic strength as well as economic strength. Indeed, the particular forum for announcement can be chosen for maximum effect—perhaps a Presidential statement at an OAS meeting, if not under more special circumstances.

[4] Written early in 1969.

Ready answers exist for possible criticisms. To the possible criticism that preferential tariff treatment for Latin America alone would be discriminatory (in comparison with treatment for other underdeveloped regions) and, hence, not in harmony with GATT principles, the answer is that the United States would be discriminating no more than the EEC area of Western Europe has *already* done in reference to the ex-colonial areas of Africa.[5] And to the possible criticism that the United States would thereby be throwing itself open to a disastrous influx of competitive output, the answer is a two-pronged one. First, a potentially troublesome influx is no near-term prospect; the industrial plant that could bring about this plight simply is not on hand. Rather, the objective in Latin America is to *create* industrial capacity; and meaningful support accorded a common market movement (by encouraging indigenous investment and by inducing foreign investment) stands to be helpful in creating this capacity. Second, at some later point, the industrial capacity that can give rise to a substantial goods inflow for the United States market *may* be present. In that event, however, Latin America will have become developed—which *is* the goal in mind. Of course, then the United States can adjust (a course not exactly new to it), or even improvise with selective protection (a course not necessarily devastating for Latin America either, once it has gotten this far). In any event, as a "political" aside, the associated problems, if arising at all, are in the future—not now.

What is important in the positive vein, by way of concluding comment, is that the proposal offers certain genuine "plus factors" for the United States, *given the alternatives* currently open to this country; and the proposal offers certain genuine "plus factors" for Latin America, given the current state of affairs there.

A LOOK AHEAD

We have argued that success *can* follow in Latin America from a common market effort, entailing certain implications. But we have not, thus far, addressed ourselves to the matter of whether success *will* follow. Viewed this way, we should frankly acknowledge, first,

[5] The "legal status" under GATT of the suggested U.S. action would be similar to that of past EEC action—though it is possible, or true, that the EEC countries had a goal in mind quite different than that implied under the proposed U.S. approach.

that prediction can be hazardous, but then modestly move to examine some factors that can help to shed light in a meaningful way.

Economists like to cite data to prove, or disprove, a point. Unfortunately, this course is not open to us in the present instance. Data of a requisite form do not exist. LACM is not even in formal operation; its status is still the technical one of "projected." And CACM and LAFTA, the "halfway" organizations enroute, have only a relatively short record. Such data as do exist appear hopefully in the right direction, but they are only fragmentary and not necessarily reflective of what might pertain under a LACM. The early stage of things simply precludes a data base likely to prove particularly informative as a guide for long-range prediction. Thus one is obliged to turn to other indicators.

In terms of attitudes, much more can be said. On the one hand, a hopeful sign is present in the progression of outlook over the years. Twenty years ago, relatively few people in Latin America were "fired up" about economic development; in the years since, the developmental urge has spread by leaps and bounds. Ten years ago, relatively few people in Latin America were "talking" economic integration; more recently, integration has become almost a password to launch conversation. Clearly, the "*Latino* disposition" is changing rather rapidly. One can only wonder what will be the nature of sentiment (of willingness to entertain expectations and to contemplate results) ten or twenty years hence. Prehaps a LACM will not have been substantially attained by 1985, as envisaged under the "Declaration of the Presidents of America." Perhaps the year 2000 will prove more realistic as a date. Whatever the case, the *direction* of things does seem unmistakable.

On the other hand, the progression in attitude has not occurred without its lapses. Recently, for example, there have been signs of a let-down in enthusiasm. Realization has dawned of how momentous are some of the problems that arise enroute and require countering. And, seeming apathy by the United States has not abetted matters either. Talk even has been heard of a need to delay formal introduction of LACM itself from the initial target date of 1970 (under the "Declaration of the Presidents of America") to 1975, ostensibly to give more time to lay the necessary groundwork.

Actually, much groundwork has been laid. Numerous actions have occurred and numerous arrangements have been instituted that, at the present stage of evolution, not only comprise "steppingstones" toward the future, but potentially act as built-in stimulators for further actions and arrangements. For example, much has been done as regards tariff restructuring on intra-regional trade, and as regards the mode of approach to such tariff restructuring. Again, the technique of "complementation agreements" has been introduced and refined. And, perhaps of foremost importance, arrangements along lines of "subregional integration" have been given form and appear to be getting under way.

A factor probably overshadowing all else in importance at the present juncture is that of the United States relationship. Firmer support by this country could have the effect of quickly revitalizing determination within Latin America. Many difficulties that seem foolhardy to tackle within a context of relative indifference from abroad could loom not nearly as forbidding if there were somewhat better reason to feel that Latin America did not, after all, stand quite so alone.

A final thought should be added in reference to the over-all perspective. The outcome of the common market movement in Latin America will not be fully known for some time. It would be hasty to conclude either "success" or "failure" at this point. To give pertinence to what we say, let us turn to an analogy, involving Russia. After the Revolution, Russia sought "economic development." Forced draft methods were invoked, and, even so, some forty years were required. The intervening years were ones of many ups and downs; and there are books on library shelves today to attest that some persons were prepared, during the 1920s and 1930s, to label the particular effort an outright failure. Yet, in the end, Russia did develop; it is well to recall that Russia was first with "sputnik."

Drawing upon the analogy in assessing the Latin American experience, we should recognize that (a) time must be allowed for, (b) the date is still early, (c) much is involved, and (d) the "final score" remains *in the future*. What we do know now is that much is at stake and that much is happening, not all good and not all bad. It just may be that someday, ten or twenty years hence, we will be able to look back to the present era and say "it was a period of great progress."

DOCUMENTS APPENDIX

DOCUMENTS APPENDIX

GATT PRINCIPLES

The historic ideal in international commercial and financial relations is "multilateralism": full latitude for the international movement of goods, free of man-made restrictions; and, as a monetary counterpart, full convertibility among national currencies. This ideal of multilateralism is basic to the spirit of the General Agreement on Tariffs and Trade (GATT), an international agreement formalized in 1947 and currently subscribed to by some sixty countries, including the United States and virtually all the countries of Latin America. Excerpts from this document appear below:[1]

ARTICLE I

Objectives

1. The contracting parties recognize that their relations in the field of trade and economic endeavour should be conducted with a view to raising standards of living, ensuring full employment and a large and steadily growing volume of real income and effective demand, developing the full use of the resources of the world and expanding the production and exchange of goods, and promoting the progressive development of the economies of all the contracting parties.

2. The contracting parties desire to contribute to these objectives through this Agreement by entering into reciprocal and mutually advantageous arrangements directed to the substantial reduction of tariffs and other barriers to trade and to the elimination of discriminatory treatment in international commerce.

ARTICLE II

General Most-Favoured-Nation Treatment

1. With respect to customs duties and charges of any kind imposed on or in connection with importation or exportation or imposed on the inter-

---

[1] From GATT, *Basic Instruments and Selected Documents* (Vol. 1, revised), Geneva, April 1955.

national transfer of payments for imports or exports, and with respect to the method of levying such duties and charges, and with respect to all rules and formalities in connection with importation and exportation, and with respect to the application of internal taxes to exported goods, . . . any advantage, favour, privilege or immunity granted by any contracting party to any product originating in or destined for any other country shall be accorded immediately and unconditionally to the like product originating in or destined for the territories of all other contracting parties. . . .

Article XXIV of GATT sets forth the conditions under which "regional integration" can comprise a permissible exception to the general rule of multilateralism.

ARTICLE XXIV

Territorial Application—Frontier Traffic—Customs Unions and Free-Trade Areas

1. The provisions of this Agreement shall apply to the metropolitan customs territories of the contracting parties and to any other customs territories in respect of which this Agreement has been accepted . . . . Each such customs territory shall, exclusively for the purposes of the territorial application of this Agreement, be treated as though it were a contracting party . . . .

2. For the purposes of this Agreement a customs territory shall be understood to mean any territory with respect to which separate tariffs or other regulations of commerce are maintained for a substantial part of the trade of such territory with other territories.

3. The provisions of this Agreement shall be construed to prevent: (a) advantages accorded by any contracting party to adjacent countries in order to facilitate frontier traffic; . . . .

4. The contracting parties recognize the desirability of increasing freedom of trade by the development, through voluntary agreements, of closer integration between the economies of the countries parties to such agreements. They also recognize that the purpose of a customs union or of a free-trade area should be to facilitate trade between the constituent territories and not to raise barriers to the trade of other contracting parties with such territories.

5. Accordingly, the provisions of this Agreement shall not prevent, as between the territories of contracting parties, the formation of a customs union or of a free-trade area or the adoption of an interim agreement necessary for the formation of a customs union or of a free-trade area;

Provided that:

(a) with respect to a customs union, or an interim agreement leading to the formation of a customs union, the duties and other regulations of commerce imposed at the institution of any such union or interim agreement in respect of trade with contracting parties not parties to such union or agreement shall not on the whole be higher or more restrictive than the general incidence of the duties and regulations of commerce applicable in the constituent territories prior to the formation of such union or the adoption of such interim agreement, as the case may be;

(b) with respect to a free-trade area, or an interim agreement leading to the formation of a free-trade area, the duties and other regulations of commerce maintained in each of the constituent territories and applicable at the formation of such free-trade area or the adoption of such interim agreement to the trade of contracting parties not included in such area or not parties to such agreement shall not be higher or more restrictive than the corresponding duties and other regulations of commerce existing in the same constituent territories prior to the formation of the free-trade area, or interim agreement, as the case may be; and

(c) any interim agreement referred to in sub-paragraphs (a) and (b) shall include a plan and schedule for the formation of such a customs union or of such a free-trade area within a reasonable length of time.

6. If, in fulfilling the requirements of sub-paragraph 5(a), a contracting party proposes to increase any rate of duty inconsistently with the provisions of Article II, the procedure set forth in Article XXVIII shall apply. In providing for compensatory adjustment, due account shall be taken of the compensation already afforded by the reductions brought about in the corresponding duty of the other constituents of the union.

7. (a) Any contracting party deciding to enter into a customs union or free-trade area, or an interim agreement leading to the formation of such a union or area, shall promptly notify the Contracting Parties and shall make available to them such information regarding the proposed union or area as will enable them to make such reports and recommendations to contracting parties as they may deem appropriate.

(b) If, after having studied the plan and schedule included in an interim agreement referred to in paragraph 5 in consultation with the parties to that agreement and taking due account of the information made available in accordance with the provisions of sub-paragraph (a), the Contracting Parties find that such agreement is not likely to result in the formation of a customs union or of a free-trade area within the period contemplated by the parties to the agreement or that such period is not a reasonable one, the Contracting Parties shall make recommendations to the parties to the agreement. The parties shall not maintain or put into force, as the case may be, such agreement if they are not prepared to modify it in accordance with these recommendations.

(c) Any substantial change in the plan or schedule referred to in paragraph 5(c) shall be communicated to the Contracting Parties, which may request the contracting parties concerned to consult with them if the change seems likely to jeopardize or delay unduly the formation of the customs union or of the free-trade area.

8. For the purposes of this Agreement:

(a) A customs union shall be understood to mean the substitution of a single customs territory for two or more customs territories, so that

(i) duties and other restrictive regulations of commerce . . . are eliminated with respect to substantially all the trade between the constituent territories of the union or at least with respect to substantially all the trade in products originating in such territories, and,

(ii) subject to the provisions of paragraph 9, substantially the same duties and other regulations of commerce are applied by each of the members of the union to the trade of territories not included in the union;

(b) A free-trade area shall be understood to mean a group of two or more customs territories in which the duties and other restrictive regulations of commerce . . . are eliminated on substantially all the trade between the constituent territories in products originating in such territories.

9. The preferences referred to in paragraph 2 of Article I shall not be affected by the formation of a customs union or of a free-trade area but may be eliminated or adjusted by means of negotiations with contracting parties affected. This procedure of negotiations with affected contracting parties shall, in particular, apply to the elimination of preferences required to conform with the provisions of paragraph 8(a)(i) and paragraph 8(b).

10. The Contracting Parties may by a two-thirds majority approve proposals which do not fully comply with the requirements of paragraphs 5 to 9 inclusive, provided that such proposals lead to the formation of a customs union or a free-trade area in the sense of this Article.

11. Taking into account the exceptional circumstances arising out of the establishment of India and Pakistan as independent States and recognizing the fact that they have long constituted an economic unit, the contracting parties agree that the provisions of this Agreement shall not prevent the two countries from entering into special arrangements with respect to the trade between them, pending the establishment of their mutual trade relations on a definitive basis.

12. Each contracting party shall take such reasonable measures as may be available to it to ensure observance of the provisions of this Agreement by the regional and local governments and authorities within its territory.

THE UNCTAD I CONFERENCE: FINAL REPORT

With two matters of special concern to underdeveloped countries—"trade" and "development"—central to its agenda, the now-famed United Nations Conference on Trade and Development (UNCTAD I) was convened in Geneva during March-June 1964. There, the confrontation between delegates from some 120 countries, developed and underdeveloped, proceeded in terms of, essentially, "underdeveloped countries versus developed countries." Reproduced below are major statements from the "Final Act," approved at the close of the sessions, June 16, 1964.[1]

GENERAL PRINCIPLES

General Principle Four

Economic development and social progress should be the common concern of the whole international community and should, by increasing economic prosperity and well-being, help strengthen peaceful relations and co-operation among nations. Accordingly, all countries pledge themselves to pursue internal and external economic policies designed to accelerate economic growth throughout the world, and in particular to help promote, in developing countries, a rate of growth consistent with the need to bring about a substantial and steady increase in average income, in order to narrow the gap between the standard of living in developing countries and that in the developed countries. . . .

General Principle Six

International trade is one of the most important factors in economic development. It should be governed by such rules as are consistent with the attainment of economic and social progress and should not be hampered by measures incompatible therewith. All countries should co-operate in creating conditions of international trade conducive, in particular, to the achievement of a rapid increase in the export earnings of developing countries and, in general, to the promotion of an expan-

---

[1] Taken and adapted from United Nations, *Proceedings of the United Nations Conference on Trade and Development* (Final Act and Report, Vol. I), New York, 1964, pp. 10–13. (Italics supplied.)

sion and diversification of trade between all countries, whether at similar levels of development, at different levels of development, or having different economic and social systems.

General Principle Seven

The expansion and diversification of international trade depends upon increasing access to markets, and upon remunerative prices for the exports of primary products. Developed countries shall progressively reduce and eliminate barriers and other restrictions that hinder trade and consumption of products from developing countries and take positive measures such as will create and increase markets for the exports of developing countries. All countries should co-operate through suitable international arrangements, on an orderly basis, in implementing measures designed to increase and stabilize primary commodity export earnings, particularly of developing countries, at equitable and remunerative prices and to maintain a mutually acceptable relationship between the prices of manufactured goods and those of primary products.

General Principle Eight

International trade should be conducted to mutual advantage on the basis of the most-favoured nation treatment and should be free from measures detrimental to the trading interests of other countries. However, *developed countries should grant concessions to all developing countries* and extend to developing countries all concessions they grant to one another *and should not, in granting these or other concessions, require any concessions in return from developing countries.* New preferential concessions, both tariff and non-tariff, should be made to developing countries as a whole and such preferences should not be extended to developed countries. *Developing countries need not extend to developed countries preferential treatment in operation amongst them.* Special preferences at present enjoyed by certain developing countries in certain developed countries should be regarded as transitional and subject to progressive reduction. They should be eliminated as and when effective international measures guaranteeing at least equivalent advantages to the countries concerned come into operation. . . .

INTERNATIONAL COMMODITY PROBLEMS

In order to deal with the problems facing the primary commodity trade of developing countries, the Conference has recommended . . . provisions . . . [for] increasing the export earnings of the developing countries by general measures as well as by specific measures related to individual commodities. . . .

TRADE IN MANUFACTURES AND SEMI-MANUFACTURES

The Conference recognizes the urgent need for the diversification and expansion of the export trade of developing countries in manufactures and semi-manufactures, as a means of accelerating their economic development and raising their standards of living. . . .

The Conference has noted both the agreement, signified by *all* developing countries and a great majority of the developed countries, with the principle of assisting the industrial development of developing countries, by the *extension of preferences in their favour,* and the opposition to this principle expressed by *some* developed countries. . . .

THE UNCTAD MOVEMENT: ASSESSMENT

The "UNCTAD movement" has given rise to two major conferences: UNCTAD I in 1964 and UNCTAD II in 1967. The following is an assessment of what has occurred.[1]

UNCTAD I

With the . . . [close of the UNCTAD I conference], what can one say in appraising apparent impact on world affairs? Certainly no great and abrupt change, politically or economically, is to be noted as having followed swiftly upon adjournment. Nevertheless, there is good reason to believe that the conference, a momentous event in and of itself, continues to hold major meaning for developments yet to come during the years ahead.

First, great significance attaches to the fact that the conference *did* occur. A global conference, convened under United Nations auspices, at which "trade and development" matters are up for discussion within the avowed context of "underdeveloped countries *versus* developed countries" is—in terms of the standards of pre-UNCTAD days—a landmark of high order. Presumably, with the firm precedent of UNCTAD now on hand, follow-up conferences, possibly even more hard-hitting, become easier to arrange.

Second, the conference revealed that a "united front" among underdeveloped countries is possible (at least when some major matters are at stake). By and large, the underdeveloped countries remained a solid bloc in the support of their initial basic position. This was no small test, and the resultant cohesion surprised many observers (who, perhaps,

---

[1] Adapted from Walter Krause, ed., *The Economy of Latin America,* University of Iowa, 1966, pp. 171–73; new material added relative to "UNCTAD II and after."

did not expect this degree of tactical sophistication from a membership embracing, among others, some countries only recently freed of a colonialist tie). And, especially this cohesion seemed remarkable with the realization that the developed countries, on their part, were *unable* to retain a fully consistent posture throughout.[2] Thus, with one demonstration of cohesion among underdeveloped countries on hand, a willingness by them to stand up in the future in a direct confrontation on other scores may be enhanced.

Third, the underdeveloped countries did not leave the conference entirely empty-handed. To illustrate, the United States offered a conciliatory policy statement to the effect that: "The industrialized nations should provide ready access to the products of the underdeveloped nations by reducing tariffs and other barriers, *without necessarily expecting full reciprocity for their own exports.*"[3] This was a far cry from the multilateralist, reciprocal-type approach to which this country had always tenaciously clung previously, and to which it had long urged other countries to subscribe. Certainly, it would prove much more difficult in the future to withstand tangible requests for action in this direction, given the fact that the statement now was on the record as a policy concession.

All in all, the UNCTAD conference represented a direct confrontation in which, clearly, the developed countries did not stand firm (or united) on all points. A reasonable presumption, thereafter, was that with a "crack in the dike" on hand for all to see, some subsequent set of circumstances of the "right" kind could well trigger the unleashing of a flood. While changes in basic ground rules typically come about only slowly, a far more tangible basis now existed for thinking that "something will have to give, sooner or later."

UNCTAD II AND AFTER

Following the UNCTAD I conference, while many concerned themselves with assessing its true significance, others, more directly involved

[2] For example, in reference to the proposal for higher tariffs by developed countries on manufactured-goods trade among themselves [as a means by which the developed countries might raise funds to "retransfer" back to the underdeveloped countries as a form of redress for the alleged long-range deterioration in the terms of trade of primary commodities—all in line with Prebisch argumentation for a "retransfer" of income], a British delegate chose to voice opposition in terms of "unfairness." He contended that those countries whose imports comprise a high percentage of GNP—Britain being a case in point—would be forced to bear a disproportionately heavy burden in the "retransfer" process. Significantly, he did *not* argue that the retransfer idea was, in itself, ill-advised (as some other developed-country groups believed). He merely questioned how the costs of the retransfer were to be shared. To onlookers, the reaction could only have been one of "something less than a united front" within the developed-countries camp.

[3] Italics supplied.

with the UNCTAD movement, promptly forged ahead with groundwork for a follow-up conference. In due course, such a further conference was scheduled, occurring in New Delhi during mid-1967.

The agenda items for UNCTAD II, as before, were "trade" and "development." Argumentation, too, proceeded in much the same way. *But* the results of UNCTAD II were less notable than those of UNCTAD I. This time the major developed countries did not seek refuge in principle to resist the "demands" of the underdeveloped countries; rather, they chose simply to argue that the time was not right to look to them in the expectation of big concessions. The United States, by way of defense for itself, cited its costly involvement in the Vietnam Conflict and its persistent balance-of-payments difficulties—which together, it suggested, currently made inappropriate concessions of the type being sought. Similarly, Great Britain cited its persistent economic difficulties, particularly its balance-of-payments difficulties—1967, in fact, being the year of a major sterling crisis. In the end, given the particular problems of the moment faced by the major countries, the underdeveloped countries were unable to push their "claims" successfully—or, more accurately perhaps, were unwilling to push to the limit with their "claims."

Thus, the UNCTAD II conference ended in a form of stalemate. The timing of the conference had been poor; though who, when scheduling two years in advance, could have foreseen accurately the environment eventually to prevail? Meanwhile, the circumstances that had triggered two conferences remained—in turn, raising other questions to await answer. Was an UNCTAD III conference to be expected at a future date? Or, were the "demands" of underdeveloped countries to be pursued in the future under a different auspices?

Not everyone was confident that the "united front" attitude of the UNCTAD movement would continue. Perhaps the unity among Latin America, Africa, and Asia .was somewhat less durable than the brief experience under the UNCTAD movement might suggest. Perhaps the more enduring attitude was more akin to the one that some Latin Americans, for example, were beginning to reflect (in substance):

> The idea of a united front between Latin America, Africa, and Asia is based on political, if not economic, unreality. We, in Latin America, see our destiny in terms of *working arrangements with the United States primarily,* just as the underdeveloped countries of Africa and Asia are logically obliged to seek their destiny in relationships geared primarily to Western Europe. Moreover, it isn't a simple case of the underdeveloped countries *versus* the developed countries (or, of Latin America *versus* the United States). Many of the raw materials of Latin America are also domestic raw materials in the United States (e.g., wheat, corn, cotton, copper, petroleum, etc.)—so that even in the problem-ridden raw-materials realm there is a substantial community of interest between Latin America *and* the United States.

If the foregoing is the view, then the applicability of an UNCTAD-type "idea" necessarily bears reorientation. Rather than a context of all underdeveloped countries vis-a-vis all developed countries, the relevant context becomes a more limited one. The context becomes that, for example, of the *particular* trading relationship between the United States and Latin America—concern being with the question of whether or not, or to what extent, the United States should offer tariff concessions on a non-reciprocal basis on manufactured-goods imports of Latin American origin, when and as these imports become a possibility in the wake of requisite development and production there.

DECLARATION OF THE PRESIDENTS OF AMERICA

Meeting in Punta del Este, Uruguay, during April 1967, the "heads of state" of the member countries of the Organization of American States joined in endorsing the "Declaration of the Presidents of America"—thereby pledging support for movement to a full-scale "Latin American" common market. Excerpts from the "Declaration" appear below:[1]

I

The Presidents of the Latin American Republics resolve to create progressively, beginning in 1970, the Latin American Common Market, which shall be substantially in operation in a period of no more than fifteen years. The Latin American Common Market will be based on the complete development and progressive convergence of the Latin American Free Trade Association and of the Central American Common Market, taking into account the interests of the Latin American countries not yet affiliated with these systems. This great task will reinforce historic bonds, will promote industrial development and the strengthening of Latin American industrial enterprises, as well as more efficient production and new opportunities for employment, and will permit the region to play its deservedly significant role in world affairs. The ties of friendship among the peoples of the Continent will thus be strengthened.

The President of the United States of America, for his part, declares his firm support for this promising Latin American initiative.

THE UNDERSIGNED PRESIDENTS AFFIRM THAT:

We will lay the physical foundations for Latin American economic integration through multinational projects.

---

[1] The full text appears in U.S. Department of State *Bulletin* (Washington, D.C., May 8, 1967), pp. 712–21.

Economic integration demands a major sustained effort to build a land transportation network and to improve transportation systems of all kinds so as to open the way for the movement of both people and goods throughout the Continent; to establish an adequate and efficient telecommunications system; to install interconnected power systems; and to develop jointly international river basins, frontier regions, and economic areas which include the territory of two or more countries.

We will join in efforts to increase substantially Latin American foreign-trade earnings.

To increase substantially Latin American foreign-trade earnings, individual and joint efforts shall be directed toward facilitating nondiscriminatory access of Latin American products in world markets, toward increasing Latin American earnings from traditional exports, toward avoiding frequent fluctuations in income from such commodities, and, finally, toward adopting measures that will stimulate exports of Latin American manufactured products. . . .

II

ACTION PROGRAM

Chapter I

LATIN AMERICAN ECONOMIC INTEGRATION AND INDUSTRIAL DEVELOPMENT

1. *Principles, objectives, and goals*

Economic integration is a collective instrument for accelerating Latin American development and should constitute one of the policy goals of each of the countries of the region. The greatest possible efforts should be made to bring it about, as a necessary complement to national development plans.

At the same time, the different levels of development and economic and market conditions of the various Latin American countries must be borne in mind, in order that the integration process may promote their harmonious and balanced growth. In this respect, the countries of relatively less economic development, and, to the extent required, those of insufficient market, will have preferential treatment in matters of trade and of technical and financial cooperation.

Integration must be fully at the service of Latin America. This requires the strengthening of Latin American enterprise through vigorous financial and technical support that will permit it to develop and supply the regional market efficiently. Foreign private enterprise will be able to fill an important function in assuring achievement of the objectives of integration within the pertinent policies of each of the countries of Latin America.

Adequate financing is required to facilitate the economic restructuring and adjustments called for by the urgent need to accelerate integration.

It is necessary to adopt all measures that will lead to the completion of Latin American integration, above all those that will bring about, in the shortest time possible, monetary stability and the elimination of all restrictions, including administrative, financial, and exchange restrictions, that obstruct the trade of the products of the area.

To these ends, the Latin American Presidents agree to take action on the following points:

a. Beginning in 1970, to establish progressively the Latin American Common Market, which should be substantially in operation within a period of no more than fifteen years.

b. The Latin American Common Market will be based on the improvement of the two existing integration systems: the Latin American Free Trade Association (LAFTA) and the Central American Common Market (CACM). The two systems will initiate simultaneously a process of convergence by stages of cooperation, closer ties, and integration, taking into account the interest of the Latin American countries not yet associated with these systems, in order to provide their access to one of them.

c. To encourage the incorporation of other countries of the Latin American region into the existing integration systems.

2. *Measures with regard to the Latin American Free Trade Association (LAFTA)*

The Presidents of the member states of LAFTA instruct their respective Ministers of Foreign Affairs, who will participate in the next meeting of the Council of Ministers of LAFTA, to be held in 1967, to adopt the measures necessary to implement the following decisions:

a. To accelerate the process of converting LAFTA into a common market. To this end, starting in 1970, and to be completed in a period of not more than fifteen years, LAFTA will put into effect a system of programmed elimination of duties and all other non-tariff restrictions, and also a system of tariff harmonization, in order to establish progressively a common external tariff at levels that will promote efficiency and productivity, as well as the expansion of trade.

b. To coordinate progressively economic policies and instruments and to harmonize national laws to the extent required for integration. These measures will be adopted simultaneously with the improvement of the integration process.

c. To promote the conclusion of sectoral agreements for industrial complementation, endeavoring to obtain the participation of the countries of relatively less economic development.

d. To promote the conclusion of temporary subregional agreements, with provision for reducing tariffs within the subregions and harmonizing treatments toward third nations more rapidly than in the general agreements, in keeping with the objectives of regional integration. Subregional tariff reductions will not be extended to countries that are not parties to the subregional agreement, nor will they create special obligations for them.

Participation of the countries of relatively less economic development in all stages of the integration process and in the formation of the Latin American Common Market will be based on the provisions of the Treaty of Montevideo and its complementary resolutions, and these countries will be given the greatest possible advantages, so that balanced development of the region may be achieved.

To this same end, they have decided to promote immediate action to facilitate free access of products of the LAFTA member countries of relatively less economic development to the market of the other LAFTA countries, and to promote the installation and financing in the former countries of industries intended for the enlarged market.

The countries of relatively less economic development will have the right to participate and to obtain preferential conditions in the subregional agreements in which they have an interest.

The situation of countries characterized as being of insufficient market shall be taken into account in temporary preferential treatments established, to the extent necessary to achieve a harmonious development in the integration process.

It is understood that all the provisions set forth in this section fall within or are based upon the Treaty of Montevideo.

3. *Measures with regard to the Central American economic integration program*

The Presidents of the member states of the Central American Common Market commit themselves:

a. To carry out an action program that will include the following measures, among others:

(1) Improvement of the customs union and establishment of a Central American monetary union;

(2) Completion of the regional network of infrastructure;

(3) Promotion of a common foreign-trade policy;

(4) Improvement of the common market in agricultural products and implementation of a joint, coordinated industrial policy;

(5) Acceleration of the process of free movement of manpower and capital within the area;

(6) Harmonization of the basic legislation required for economic integration.

b. To apply, in the implementation of the foregoing measures, and when pertinent, the temporary preferential treatment already established or that may be established, in accordance with the principle of balanced development among countries.

c. To foster closer ties between Panama and the Central American Common Market, as well as rapid expansion of trade and investment relations with neighboring countries of the Central American and Caribbean region, taking advantage, to this end, of their geographic proximity and of the possibilities for economic complementation; also, to seek conclusion of subregional agreements and agreements of industrial complementation between Central America and other Latin American countries.

4. *Measures common to Latin American countries*

The Latin American Presidents commit themselves:

a. Not to establish new restrictions on trade among Latin American countries, except in special cases, such as those arising from equalization of tariffs and other instruments of trade policy, as well as from the need to assure the initiation or expansion of certain productive activities in countries of relatively less economic development.

b. To establish, by a tariff cut or other equivalent measures, a margin of preference within the region for all products originating in Latin American countries, taking into account the different degrees of development of the countries.

c. To have the measures in the two preceding paragraphs applied immediately among the member countries of LAFTA, in harmony with the other measures referring to this organization contained in the present chapter and, insofar as possible, to extend them to nonmember countries in a manner compatible with existing international commitments, inviting the latter countries to extend similar preference to the members of LAFTA, with the same qualification.

d. To ensure that application of the foregoing measures shall not hinder internal readjustments designed to rationalize the instruments of trade policy made necessary in order to carry out national development plans and to achieve the goals of integration.

e. To promote acceleration of the studies already initiated regarding preferences that LAFTA countries might grant to imports from the Latin American countries that are not members of the Association.

f. To have studies made of the possibility of concluding agreements of industrial complementation in which all Latin American countries may participate, as well as temporary subregional economic integration agreements between the CACM and member countries of LAFTA.

g. To have a committee established composed of the executive organs of LAFTA and the CACM to coordinate implementation of the foregoing points. To this end, the committee will encourage meetings at the ministerial level, in order to ensure that Latin American integration will proceed as rapidly as possible, and, in due course, initiate negotiation of a general treaty or the protocols required to create the Latin American Common Market. Latin American countries that are not members shall be invited to send representatives to these meetings and to those of the committee of the executive organs of LAFTA and the CACM.

h. To give special attention to industrial development within integration, and particularly to the strengthening of Latin American industrial firms. In this regard, we reiterate that development must be balanced between investments for economic ends and investments for social ends.

5. *Measures common to member countries of the Organization of American States (OAS)*

The Presidents of the member states of the OAS agree:

a. To mobilize financial and technical resources within and without the hemisphere to contribute to the solution of problems in connection with the balance of payments, industrial readjustments, and retraining of the labor force that may arise from a rapid reduction of trade barriers during the period of transition toward the common market, as well as to increase the sums available for export credits in intra-Latin American trade. The Inter-American Development Bank and the organs of both existing integration systems should participate in the mobilization of such resources.

b. To mobilize public and private resources within and without the hemisphere to encourage industrial development as part of the integration process and of national development plans.

c. To mobilize financial and technical resources to undertake specific feasibility studies on multinational projects for Latin American industrial firms, as well as to aid in carrying out these projects.

d. To accelerate the studies being conducted by various inter-American agencies to promote strengthening of capital markets and the possible establishment of a Latin American stock market.

e. To make available to Central America, within the Alliance for Progress, adequate technical and financial resources, including those required for strengthening and expanding the existing Central American Economic Integration Fund, for the purpose of accelerating the Central American economic integration program.

f. To make available, within the Alliance for Progress and pursuant to the provisions of the Charter of Punta del Este, the technical and financial resources needed to accelerate the preparatory studies and work involved in converting LAFTA into a common market.

Chapter II

MULTINATIONAL ACTION FOR INFRASTRUCTURE PROJECTS

The economic integration of Latin America demands a vigorous and sustained effort to complete and modernize the physical infrastructure of the region. It is necessary to build a land transport network and improve all types of transport systems to facilitate the movement of persons and goods throughout the hemisphere; to establish an adequate and efficient telecommunications system and inter-connected power systems; and jointly to develop international watersheds, frontier regions and economic areas that include the territory of two or more countries. In Latin America there are in existence projects in all these fields, at different stages of preparation or implementation, but in many cases the completion of prior studies, financial resources, or merely the coordination of efforts and the decision to bring them to fruition are lacking.

The Presidents of the member states of the OAS agree to engage in determined action to undertake or accelerate the construction of the infrastructure required for the development and integration of Latin America and to make better use thereof. In so doing, it is essential that the groups of interested countries or multinational institutions determine criteria for assigning priorities, in view of the amount of human and material resources needed for the task.

As one basis for the criteria, which will be determined with precision upon consideration of the specific cases submitted for study, they stress the fundamental need to give preferential attention to those projects that benefit the countries of the region that are at a relatively lower level of economic development.

Priority should also be given to the mobilization of financial and technical resources for the preparation and implementation of infrastructure projects that will facilitate the participation of landlocked countries in regional and international trade.

In consequence, they adopt the following decisions for immediate implementation:

1. To complete the studies and conclude the agreements necessary to accelerate the construction of an inter-American telecommunications network.

2. To expedite the agreements necessary to complete the Pan American Highway, to accelerate the construction of the Bolivarian Highway (Carretera Marginal de la Selva) and its junction with the Trans-Chaco Highway and to support the studies and agreements designed to bring into being the new highway systems that will join groups of countries of continental and insular Latin America, as well as the basic works required to develop water and airborne transport of a multinational nature and the corresponding systems of operation. As a complement to these agreements, negotiations should be undertaken for the purpose of eliminating or reducing to a minimum the restrictions on international traffic and of promoting technical and administrative cooperation among land, water, and air transport enterprises and the establishment of multinational transport services.

3. To sponsor studies for preparing joint projects in connection with watersheds, such as the studies commenced on the development of the River Plate basin and that relating to the Gulf of Fonseca.

4. To allocate sufficient resources to the Preinvestment Fund for Latin American Integration of the IDB for conducting studies that will make it possible to identify and prepare multinational projects in all fields that may be of importance in promoting regional integration. In order that the aforesaid Fund may carry out an effective promotion effort, it is necessary that an adequate part of the resources allocated may be used without reimbursement, or with reimbursement conditioned on the execution of the corresponding projects.

5. To mobilize, within and outside the hemisphere, resources in addition to those that will continue to be placed at the disposal of the countries to support national economic development programs, such resources to be devoted especially to the implementation of multinational infrastructure projects that can represent important advances in the Latin American economic integration process. In this regard, the IDB should have additional resources in order to participate actively in the attainment of this objective.

Chapter III

MEASURES TO IMPROVE INTERNATIONAL TRADE CONDITIONS IN LATIN AMERICA

The economic development of Latin America is seriously affected by the adverse conditions in which its international trade is carried out. Market structures, financial conditions, and actions that prejudice exports and other income from outside Latin America are impeding its growth and retarding the integration process. All this causes particular concern in view of the serious and growing imbalance between the standard of living in Latin American countries and that of the industrialized nations and, at the same time, calls for definite decisions and adequate instruments to implement the decisions.

Individual and joint efforts of the member states of the OAS are essential to increase the incomes of Latin American countries derived from, and to avoid frequent fluctuations in, traditional exports, as well as to promote new exports. Such efforts are also essential to reduce any adverse effects on the external earnings of Latin American countries that may be caused by measures which may be taken by industrialized countries for balance of payments reasons.

The Charter of Punta del Este, the Economic and Social Act of Rio de Janeiro and the new provisions of the Charter of the OAS reflect a hemispheric agreement with regard to these problems, which needs to be effectively implemented; therefore, the Presidents of the member states of the OAS agree:

1. To act in coordination in multilateral negotiations to achieve,

without the more highly developed countries' expecting reciprocity, the greatest possible reduction or the elimination of tariffs and other restrictions that impede the access of Latin American products to world markets. The Government of the United States intends to make efforts for the purpose of liberalizing the conditions affecting exports of basic products of special interest to Latin American countries, in accordance with the provisions of Article 37(a) of the Protocol of Buenos Aires.

2. To consider together possible systems of general nonreciprocal preferential treatment for exports of manufactures and semimanufactures of the developing countries, with a view to improving the condition of the Latin American export trade.

3. To undertake a joint effort in all international institutions and organizations to eliminate discriminatory preferences against Latin American exports.

4. To strengthen the system of intergovernmental consultations and carry them out sufficiently in advance, so as to render them effective and ensure that programs for placing and selling surpluses and reserves that affect the exports of the developing countries take into account the interests of the Latin American countries.

5. To ensure compliance with international commitments to refrain from introducing or increasing tariff and nontariff barriers that affect exports of the developing countries, taking into account the interests of Latin America.

6. To combine efforts to strengthen and perfect existing international agreements, particularly the International Coffee Agreement, to obtain favorable conditions for trade in basic products of interest to Latin America and to explore all possibilities for the development of new agreements.

7. To support the financing and prompt initiation of the activities of the Coffee Diversification Fund, and consider in due course the creation of other funds to make it possible to control the production of basic products of interest to Latin America in which there is a chronic imbalance between supply and demand.

8. To adopt measures to make Latin American export products more competitive in world markets.

9. To put in operation as soon as possible an inter-American agency for export promotion that will help to identify and develop new export lines and to strengthen the placing of Latin American products in international markets, and to improve national and regional agencies designed for the same purpose.

10. To initiate such individual or joint action on the part of the member states of the OAS as may be required to ensure effective and timely execution of the foregoing agreements, as well as those that may be required to continue the execution of the agreements contained in the Charter of Punta del Este, in particular those relating to foreign trade. . . .

STATISTICAL APPENDIX

STATISTICAL APPENDIX

Table 1. *Diversity Among Latin American Countries, 1968*

	Countries	Area (sq. mi.)	Population (thous.)	GNP[1] (mill. $ U.S.)	Per-Capita GNP[1] ($ U.S.)
LAFTA	*More Developed*				
	Argentina	1,072,109	23,617	15,650	668
	Brazil	3,286,600	88,209	31,650	359
	Mexico	759,559	47,276	25,820	546
	Lesser Developed				
	Insufficient Market				
	Chile	292,268	9,351	5,600	610
	Colombia	439,530	19,825	5,872	296
	Peru	494,312	12,772	4,055	318
	Uruguay	72,175	2,818	1,483	525
	Venezuela	347,042	9,686	8,890	928
	Relatively Less Developed				
	Bolivia	424,179	4,680	760	171
	Ecuador	104,510	5,695	1,420	253
	Paraguay	157,053	2,231	498	224
CACM	Costa Rica	19,653	1,640	720	436
	El Salvador	8,083	3,266	912	286
	Guatemala	42,044	4,864	1,487	293
	Honduras	43,277	2,413	606	240
	Nicaragua	53,670	1,842	677	367
OTHER	Panama	29,210	1,372	815	594
	Dom. Rep.	18,704	4,029	1,111	276
	Haiti	10,715	4,671	370	78

[1] Constant 1967 prices.

Source: Column 1 from UCLA (Latin American Center), *Statistical Abstract of Latin America 1967* (Los Angeles, December 1968), p. 48; column 2 from UN, *Monthly Bulletin of Statistics*, New York, May 1969, pp. 1–5; columns 3 and 4 from AID, *Gross National Product*, Washington, April 1969, pp. 8–9.

Table 2. *Industrial and Transportation Data for Latin America, 1967*

	Countries	Degree of Industrialization[1] (percent)	Cement Prod. (thous. met. tons)	Crude Steel Manufacturing (thous. met. tons)
LAFTA	*More Developed*			
	Argentina	33.4	3,492	1,288
	Brazil	24.0	6,002	3,532
	Mexico	26.1	4,966	2,645
	Lesser Developed *Insufficient Market*			
	Chile	24.4	1,362	556
	Colombia	18.6	2,075	216
	Peru	16.5	1,021	82
	Uruguay	21.2	432	12
	Venezuela	14.6	2,063	632
	Relatively Less Developed			
	Bolivia	14.5	61	. . .
	Ecuador	17.4	325	. . .
	Paraguay	16.1	27	. . .
CACM	Costa Rica	13.8	115	. . .
	El Salvador	18.1	143	. . .
	Guatemala	14.3	202	. . .
	Honduras	14.4	103	. . .
	Nicaragua	13.7	67	. . .
OTHER	Panama	16.3	165	. . .
	Dom. Rep.	16.5	229	. . .
	Haiti	. . .	55	. . .

[1] Percentage relation between industrial (manufacturing) GDP and total GDP.

Source: Column 1 from AID, *Latin America: Economic Growth Trends,* Washington, D.C., December 1968, p. 16; columns 2–9 developed from UCLA (Latin American Center), *Statistical Abstract of Latin America 1967* (Los Angeles, December 1968), UN, *Monthly Bulletin of Statistics,* New York, May 1969, and from information supplied by AID, Statistics and Reports Division, and PAU, Statistical Office.

Electrical Energy Prod. (mill. KWH)	Motor Vehicles (thous.)	Paved Roads (mi.)	Railroads (thous. mi.)	Air Transport (mill. ton/mi.)	Merchant Fleet (thous. gross tons
15,420	1,737	22,000	44	88	1,361
32,654	2,236	18,730	37	260	1,501
19,399	1,290	37,321	25	115	380
6,670	203	6,664	8	41	369
6,355	245	6,692	3	115	210
4,085	286	4,932	4	24	197
1,720	251	2,736	3	6	160
8,900	580	16,431	1	49	377
620	45	615	4	5	...
700	49	1,771	1	5	43
205	22	430	1	2	21
855	41	1,210	1	15	92
475	41	1,176	1	11	...
520	63	1,595	1	6	...
200	20	415	1	8	90
335	25	1,049	...	5	...
510	44	1,360	1	8	...
715	47	4,757	2	1	27
110	8	420	...	...	...

Table 3. *Trends in LAFTA Trade, 1960–1968*[1]

Year	Exports (fob)	Imports (cif)	Total	Percentage relative index (1961 = 100)	Percentage change from preceding period	Percent of total LAFTA trade
	(mill. $ U.S.)					
			Intrazonal			
1960	340.1	375.1	715.2	109		6.9
1961	298.7	359.9	658.7	100	—9	6.1
			Treaty of Montevideo			
1962	352.8	419.6	772.4	117	17	7.0
1963	425.2	506.0	931.2	141	24	8.4
1964	555.5	645.2	1,200.7	182	41	10.1
1965	635.2	771.5	1,406.7	214	32	11.4
1966	675.2	781.9	1,457.1	221	7	10.6
1967	651.1	764.2	1,415.3	215	—6	10.3
1968[2]	756.0	848.0	1,604.0	244	29	11.1
			Extrazonal			
1960	4,393.4	5,313.3	9,706.7	95		93.1
1961	4,491.5	5,662.9	10,154.4	100	5	93.9
1962	4,693.1	5,516.9	10,209.9	101	1	93.0
1963	5,037.7	5,165.2	10,202.9	100	—1	91.6
1964	5,387.8	5,347.7	10,735.5	106	6	89.9
1965	5,714.1	5,242.2	10,956.3	108	2	88.6
1966	6,239.3	6,079.2	12,318.5	121	13	89.4
1967	6,062.3	6,311.3	12,373.6	122	1	89.7
1968[2]	6,141.4	6,789.4	12,930.8	127	5	88.9
			Total			
1960	4,733.5	5,688.4	10,421.9	95		100.
1961	4,790.2	6,022.8	10,813.0	100	5	100.
1962	5,045.9	5,936.4	10,982.3	102	2	100.
1963	5,462.8	5,671.2	11,134.0	103	1	100.
1964	5,943.3	5,992.9	11,936.2	110	7	100.
1965	6,349.3	6,013.7	12,363.0	114	4	100.
1966	6,914.5	6,861.0	13,775.5	127	13	100.
1967	6,713.4	7,075.4	13,788.8	128	1	100.
1968[2]	6,897.4	7,637.4	14,534.8	134	6	100.

[1] Excludes Bolivia and Venezuela.

[2] Estimates.

Source: Adapted from LAFTA (Comite Ejecutivo Permanente), *El Comercio Exterior de la ALALC* (CEP/Repartido), Montevideo, 1969, p. 4.

Table 4. *Tariff Concessions Within LAFTA, 1962–1969*

	1962	%	1963	Cum.	%	1964	Cum.	%	1965	Cum.	%	1966	Cum.	%	1967	Cum.	%	1968	Cum.	%	1969	Cum.	%
More Developed																							
Argentina	414	12.7	658	1072	14.1	208	1280	15.5	83	1363	16.1	174	1537	17.0	84	1621	17.3	96	1717	16.5	122	1839	16.9
Brazil	619	19.0	631	1250	16.5	62	1312	15.9	40	1352	16.0	159	1511	16.7	92	1603	17.1	107	1710	16.5	92	1802	16.6
Mexico	288	8.9	319	607	8.0	120	727	8.8	75	802	9.5	135	937	10.4	93	1030	11.0	60	1090	10.5	83	1173	10.8
Lesser Developed																							
Insufficient Market																							
Chile	343	10.6	490	833	11.0	31	864	10.5	8	872	10.3	22	894	9.9	23	917	9.7	42	959	9.2	11	970	8.9
Colombia	268	8.3	351	619	8.1	85	704	8.5	10	714	8.4	31	745	8.2	6	751	8.0	15	766	7.4	11	777	7.2
Peru	227	7.0	72	299	3.9	56	355	4.3	9	364	4.3	28	392	4.3	10	402	4.3	22	424	4.1	46	470	4.3
Uruguay	567	17.5	43	610	8.0	54	664	8.1	0	664	7.8	12	676	7.4	13	689	7.3	27	716	6.9	68	784	7.2
Venezuela	...	...	...	...	...	...	...	...	...	...	...	...	...	...	...	...	...	438	438	4.2	6	444	4.1
Relatively Less Developed																							
Bolivia	...	...	...	...	...	...	...	...	...	...	...	...	...	...	...	...	...	178	178	1.7	16	194	1.8
Ecuador	...	...	1714	1714	22.6	—37	1677	20.3	3	1680	19.8	5	1685	18.6	4	1689	18.0	8	1697	16.4	23	1720	15.8
Paraguay	520	16.0	69	589	7.8	76	665	8.1	—2	663	7.8	14	677	7.5	14	691	7.3	0	691	6.6	5	696	6.4
Total	3246	100	4347	7593	100	655	8248	100	226	8474	100	580	9054	100	339	9343	100	993	10386	100	483	10869	100

Source: Adapted from LAFTA (Comite Ejecutivo Permanente), *El Comercio Exterior de la ALALC* (CEP/Repartido 1161), Montevideo, 1969, p. 25.

Table 5. *Tariff Concessions and Intrazonal Trade Within LAFTA, 1964*

Product	Percent of Zonal Imports	Percent of LAFTA Tariff Concessions	Percent of LAFTA Tariff Concessions on Products Weighted by Products Share of Total Zonal Imports
Animals and products	9	4.5	0.4
Vegetable products	35	7.5	2.6
Fats and oils	3	3.0	0.1
Industrial food products	8	4.5	0.4
Mineral products	3	4.5	0.1
Chemical products	5	24.5	1.2
Plastics, resins, synthetics, rubber	2	2.0	0.0
Hides and skins and their manufacture	x[1]	1.0	0.0
Wool and products	8	3.5	0.3
Paper and materials	2	2.0	0.0
Textiles	10	2.0	0.2
Shoes, hats, etc.	x	x	0.0
Ceramics, stone, glass, etc.	x	1.5	0.0
Precious stones, etc.	x	x	0.0
Common metals and manufactures	10	10.0	0.1
Machinery and equipment	3	22.0	0.1
Transport products	x	1.5	0.0
Instruments	x	4.0	0.0
Arms and munitions	x	x	0.0
Miscellaneous	x	x	0.0
Art objects	x	x	0.0
Total	95	98.0	

[1] X represents magnitudes of under 1 percent.

Source: W. V. Turnage, *LAFTA 1966 in Review* (Montevideo, 1966); mimeographed report.

Table 6. *Distribution of Intrazonal Trade Among LAFTA Countries, 1952–1968* (percentages)

Countries	1952/61	1961	Treaty of Montevideo 1962	1963	1964	1965	1966	1967	1968
More Developed									
Argentina	36.2	34.3	31.6	30.2	32.3	34.7	32.2	34.1	34.8
Brazil	28.8	21.2	26.3	25.2	25.0	27.6	23.9	23.1	24.6
Mexico	1.0	1.8	3.0	3.9	4.2	4.7	6.2	6.1	5.6
Lesser Developed									
Insufficient Market									
Chile	13.4	19.6	15.5	17.8	15.2	12.5	13.2	15.6	13.8
Colombia	1.8	2.4	2.6	2.8	3.7	3.9	5.9	3.6	4.3
Peru	8.1	9.4	12.1	11.8	10.2	9.6	9.9	9.0	8.8
Uruguay	6.7	6.0	5.4	4.9	5.3	3.4	4.9	4.3	3.9
Relatively Less Developed									
Ecuador	1.4	1.8	1.3	1.4	1.7	1.6	1.4	1.9	2.2
Paraguay	2.6	3.0	2.2	2.0	2.2	2.0	2.4	2.3	2.0
	100	100	100	100	100	100	100	100	100

Source: LAFTA (Comite Ejecutivo Permanente), *El Comercio Exterior de la ALALC* (CEP/Repartido 1161), Montevideo, 1969, p. 6.

Table 7. *Trade Balances Within LAFTA, 1961–1968*
(millions of U.S. dollars)

		More Developed			Insufficient Market				Relatively Less Developed	
		Argentina	Brazil	Mexico	Chile	Colombia	Peru	Uruguay	Ecuador	Paraguay
	Exports	100.0	95.2	7.9	34.8	6.1	31.5	5.8	7.5	9.9
1961	Imports	126.0	45.2	4.1	94.5	10.2	31.8	34.5	4.1	9.8
	Balance	−26.0	+50.0	+3.8	−59.7	−4.1	−0.3	−28.7	+3.4	+0.1
	Exports	141.4	75.8	16.7	39.4	7.3	48.8	8.0	6.1	10.9
1962	Imports	103.2	128.6	6.1	80.6	12.5	45.2	34.0	3.9	6.0
	Balance	+38.2	−52.8	+10.6	−41.2	−5.2	+3.6	−26.0	+2.2	+4.9
	Exports	185.0	76.0	25.9	49.3	6.1	49.1	15.0	8.0	10.7
1963	Imports	101.6	163.9	10.8	120.0	21.4	62.0	31.7	5.2	8.4
	Balance	+83.4	−87.9	+15.1	−70.7	−15.3	−12.9	−16.7	+2.8	+2.3
	Exports	218.4	132.8	34.0	54.5	11.1	65.5	15.0	11.1	14.5
1964	Imports	170.7	168.0	17.3	128.9	33.1	58.9	48.3	7.6	11.6
	Balance	+47.7	−35.2	+16.7	−74.4	−22.0	+6.6	−33.3	+3.5	+2.9
	Exports	231.1	197.4	36.3	153.2	16.7	54.1	15.6	13.2	17.5
1965	Imports	255.7	190.4	29.7	122.1	38.3	80.9	32.1	10.0	13.3
	Balance	−24.4	+7.0	+6.6	−68.9	−21.6	−26.8	−16.5	+3.2	+4.2
	Exports	242.7	181.5	56.7	53.7	29.1	52.3	26.7	12.5	19.9
1966	Imports	226.7	167.0	33.7	140.9	56.0	91.5	46.0	8.3	14.3
	Balance	+16.0	+14.5	+23.0	−87.2	−26.9	−39.2	−19.3	+4.2	+5.6
	Exports	271.4	154.2	47.7	77.4	18.8	34.2	17.0	14.8	15.6
1967	Imports	212.0	171.6	38.2	143.1	31.9	93.4	44.1	12.4	16.5
	Balance	+59.4	−17.4	+9.5	−65.7	−13.1	−59.2	−27.1	+2.4	−0.9
	Exports	318.0	186.0	50.0	86.1	25.3	43.0	4.6	19.0	16.0
1968[1]	Imports	239.0	210.0	41.0	147.8	36.4	98.0	19.8	17.0	17.0
	Balance	+79.0	−24.0	+9.0	−61.7	−11.1	−55.0	−15.2	+2.0	−1.0
Total balance 1961–1968		+273.0	−145.8	+94.3	−529.5	−119.3	−183.2	−182.8	+23.7	−18.1
Percentage increase in exports 1961–1968		218.0	95.4	532.9	147.4	314.8	36.5	−20.7	153.3	61.6
Percentage increase in imports 1961–1968		89.7	364.6	900.0	56.4	256.8	208.2	−42.6	314.6	73.5

[1] Data for Uruguay and Ecuador based on the period January–June 1968.

Source: Adapted from LAFTA, *Síntesis Mensual*, Montevideo, February 1968, pp. 86–87, and November 1968, p. 484, and LAFTA (Comite Ejecutivo Permanente), *El Comercio Exterior de la ALALC* (CEP/ Repartido 1161), Montevideo, 1969, p. 14.

Table 8. *Complementation Agreements Within LAFTA*

Agreement Number	Sector	Date of Subscription	Participants	Statement of Compatibility	Date Activated
1	Statistical machines	July 20, 1962	Argentina, Brazil, Chile, and Uruguay	Resolution 21, CEP Aug. 10, 1962	Chile–Aug. 24, 1962 Brazil–Oct. 11, 1962 Uruguay–Oct. 31, 1962 Argentina–Nov. 27, 1962
2	Electronic tubes	Feb. 18, 1964	Argentina, Brazil, Chile, Mexico, and Uruguay	Resolution 42, CEP March 19, 1964	Brazil–May 7, 1964 Argentina–May 27, 1964 Chile–Nov. 18, 1964 Uruguay–June 17, 1964 Mexico–June 23, 1964
3	Household electrical appliances	June 2, 1966	Brazil and Uruguay	Resolution 94, CEP July 1, 1966	Uruguay–July 14, 1966 Brazil–Oct. 12, 1966
4	Electronic and electrical communications equipment	June 2, 1966	Brazil and Uruguay	Resolution 94, CEP July 1, 1966	Uruguay–Sept. 9, 1966 Brazil–Oct. 12, 1966
5	Products of the chemical industry	Dec. 19, 1967	Argentina, Brazil, Colombia, Chile, Mexico, Peru, Uruguay, and Venezuela	Resolution 142, CEP April 5, 1968	Colombia–July 19, 1968 Peru–July 26, 1968 Chile–Aug. 7, 1968 Brazil–Aug. 21, 1968 Argentina– Uruguay– Venezuela–
6	Products of the petro-chemical industry	July 25, 1968	Bolivia, Colombia, Chile, and Peru	Resolution 154, CEP Aug. 29, 1968	Bolivia– Colombia– Chile– Peru–
7	Products of the household goods industry	Aug. 27, 1968	Argentina and Uruguay	Resolution 157, CEP Sept. 24, 1968	Argentina– Uruguay–

Source: LAFTA, *Síntesis Mensual,* Montevideo, November 1968, pp. 506–507.

Table 9. *Trade Impact of Complementation Agreements Within LAFTA, 1962–1966*

Sector	Participants	Imports of Products Included in the Agreement (mill. $ U.S.)					Source of Imports of Products Included in the Agreement (mill. $ U.S.)				
		1962	1963	1964	1965	1966	1962	1963	1964	1965	1966
Statistical machines	Argentina	1.9	0.4	33.6	254.3	196.8	1.3	356.5	611.6	767.2	991.2
	Brazil	...	319.9	280.9	473.6	654.4	1.9	....	33.6	301.4	343.5
	Chile	...	....	276.3	304.8	469.9	...	....	....	....	0.6
	Uruguay	1.3	36.6	54.4	35.9	14.2	...	0.4	....	....	....
	Total	3.2	356.9	645.2	1068.6	1335.3	3.2	356.9	645.2	1068.6	1335.3
Electronic tubes	Argentina	...	....	128.0	1218.4	1548.7	...	....	4.3	5.3	47.0
	Brazil	...	....	4.0	4.3	33.8	...	....	31.1	849.6	601.8
	Mexico	...	....	....	....	54.7	...	....	....	22.5	718.5
	Chile	...	....	6.9	3.3	33.5	...	....	96.9	322.3	275.0
	Uruguay	...	....	....	0.2	....	...	....	6.9	26.5	28.4
	Total	...	....	139.2	1226.2	1670.7	...	....	139.2	1226.2	1670.7
Electronic and electrical	Brazil	...	....	....	....	47.6	...	....	....	....	....
	Uruguay	...	....	....	....	n.a.	...	....	....	....	....
communications							...	....	....	....	....
equipment	Total	...	....	....	....	47.6					

Source: Adapted from LAFTA. *Sintesis Mensual*, Montevideo, February 1968, pp. 62–68.

Table 10. *Net Balances of Multilateral Compensation Under LAFTA, 1967–1969*[1]

Countries	Debtors						Creditors					
	1967		1968		1969		1967		1968		1969	
	Total	Percent	Total	Percent	Total	Percent	Total	Percent	Total	Percent	Total	Percent
More Developed												
Argentina							15,955	83	21,252	83	14,010	65
Mexico							2,886	15	4,453	17	7,596	35
Lesser Developed												
Insufficient Market												
Chile	10,085	53	12,013	47	8,239	38						
Colombia			2,792	11	1,733	8	319	2				
Peru	8,304	43	8,679	33	8,509	39						
Relatively Less Developed												
Bolivia			448	2	932	4						
Ecuador	718	4	475	2	2,059	10						
Paraguay	53		1,298	5	111	1						
Total	19,160	100	25,705	100	21,607	100	19,160	100	25,705	100	21,607	100

[1] Net balances of respective central banks in thousands of U.S. dollars. Data for 1967–1968 cover to the second period of negotiations and, for 1969, to the first period of negotiations.

Source: Adapted from LAFTA, *Síntesis Mensual,* Montevideo, July 1967, November 1968, and May 1969.

Table 11. *Price Movements Within LAFTA Countries, 1961–1968*
(percentage increase from end of previous year)

Countries	1961	1963	1965	1966	1967	1968
More Developed						
Argentina	19.0	27.7	38.3	30.0	33.0	10.0
Brazil	43.4	81.2	41.1	46.1	27.0	25.0
Mexico	—2.8	0.0	4.5	4.3	2.0	2.0
Lesser Developed						
Insufficient Market						
Chile	9.2	45.4	25.7	17.1	17.0	28.0
Colombia	5.4	46.0	15.1	14.1	8.0	6.0
Peru	6.7	9.7	15.8	8.4	13.0	10.0
Uruguay	10.4	44.0	88.0	49.8	64.0	66.0
Venezuela	0.9	1.0	4.8	0.0	2.0	1.0
Relatively Less Developed						
Bolivia	7.4	—1.5	4.8	11.2	3.0	3.0
Ecuador	2.9	5.4	5.8	3.1	6.2	3.0
Paraguay[1]	18.5	2.1	4.1	2.6	...	3.0

[1] Increases in yearly averages.

Source: IMF, *International Financial Statistics,* Washington, D.C., various issues.

Table 12. *Currency Fluctuations Among LAFTA Countries, 1962–1968*
(national currency per U.S. dollar; mid-point rates)

Countries	1962	1963	1964	1965	1966	1967	1968
More Developed							
Argentina	134.10	132.50	150.90	188.50	247.30	350.00	350.00
Brazil	475.0	620.0	1,850.0	2,220.0	2,220.0	2.715	3.220
Mexico	12.49	12.49	12.49	12.49	12.49	12.49	12.49
Lesser Developed							
Insufficient Market							
Chile	1.64	2.15	2.70	3.43	4.37	5.79	6.66
Colombia	9.00	9.00	9.00	13.51	13.50	15.82	16.32
Peru	26.82	26.82	26.82	26.82	26.82	38.70	38.70
Uruguay	.....	17.35	24.35	69.20	76.50	199.00	250.00
Venezuela	3.35	3.35	4.50	4.50	4.50	4.50	4.50
Relatively Less Developed							
Bolivia	11.885	11.88	11.88	11.88	11.88	11.88	11.88
Ecuador	22.10	18.53	18.52	18.52	20.48	19.96	22.21
Paraguay	126.0	126.0	126.0	126.0	126.0	126.0	126.0

Source: UCLA (Latin American Center), *Statistical Abstract of Latin America 1967* (Los Angeles, December 1968), p. 189.

Table 13. *Trends in CACM Trade, 1960–1967*

Year	Exports (fob)	Imports (cif)	Total	Percentage relative index (1961 = 100)	Percentage change from preceding period	Percent of total CACM trade
	(mill. $ U.S.)					
			Intrazonal			
1960	32.6	32.6	65.2	87		5.9
			Treaty of Managua			
1961	36.8	36.8	73.6	100	11	6.6
1962	50.8	50.8	101.6	138	38	7.9
1963	72.1	72.1	144.2	196	56	9.7
1964	106.2	106.2	212.4	289	113	12.4
1965	135.5	135.5	271.0	368	79	13.9
1966	173.2	173.2	346.4	495	127	16.4
1967	213.6	213.6	427.2	580	85	19.4
			Extrazonal			
1960	433.4	609.4	1,042.8	99		94.1
1961	443.2	605.2	1,048.4	100	1	93.4
1962	507.2	671.2	1,178.4	112	12	92.1
1963	573.9	771.9	1,345.8	128	16	90.3
1964	635.8	858.8	1,494.6	142	14	87.6
1965	702.5	978.5	1,681.0	160	18	86.1
1966	752.8	1,015.8	1,768.6	169	9	83.6
1967	723.4	1,055.4	1,778.8	170	1	80.0
			Total			
1960	466.0	642.0	1,108.0	99		100.
1961	480.0	642.0	1,122.0	100	1	100.
1962	558.0	722.0	1,280.0	114	14	100.
1963	646.0	844.0	1,490.0	133	19	100.
1964	742.0	965.0	1,707.0	152	19	100.
1965	838.0	1,114.0	1,952.0	174	22	100.
1966	926.0	1,189.0	2,115.0	188	14	100.
1967	937.0	1,269.0	2,206.0	197	9	100.

Source: Calculated from export and import data in SIECA, *Carta Informativa* (Statistical Annex–77), Guatemala City, August 12, 1968; and UCLA (Latin American Center), *Statistical Abstract of Latin America 1967* (Los Angeles, December 1968), p. 206.

BIBLIOGRAPHY

BIBLIOGRAPHY

A list of publications, selective in coverage, is included to assist those readers who may wish to survey additional materials. The publications are arranged under broad headings, and are grouped as books (including also major monographs), articles, and documents (government, international agency, and other).

GENERAL REFERENCES

BOOKS:

Balassa, Bela. *Economic Development and Integration.* Mexico City: Centro de Estudios Monetarios Latinoamëricanos, 1965.

de Oliveira Campos, Roberto. *Reflections on Latin American Development.* University of Texas Press, 1967.

Castillo, Carlos M. *Growth and Integration in Central America.* New York: Frederick A. Praeger, 1967.

Currie, Lauchlin. *Accelerating Development.* New York: McGraw-Hill Book Co., 1966.

Dell, Sidney. *A Latin American Common Market?* New York: Oxford University Press, 1966.

Ellis, Howard S., and Wallich, Henry C., eds. *Economic Development for Latin America.* New York: St. Martin's Press, 1961.

Furtado, Celso. *Development and Underdevelopment.* Berkeley: University of California Press, 1964.

Glade, William P. *The Latin American Economies.* New York: Van Nostrand, 1969.

Gordon, Wendell C. *The Political Economy of Latin America.* New York: Columbia University Press, 1965.

Grunwald, Joseph, ed. *Latin American Integration: Methodological Essays.* Washington: The Brookings Institution, 1968.

Haas, Ernest B., and Schmitter, Philippe C. *The Politics of Economics in Latin American Regionalism.* University of Denver: The Social Science Foundation and Graduate School of International Studies, 1965–1966.

Hansen, Roger D. *Central America: Regional Integration and Economic Development.* Washington: National Planning Association, 1967.

Herrera, Felipe. *América Latina Integrada.* Buenos Aires: Losada, 1964.

Hilton, Ronald, ed. *The Movement Toward Latin American Unity.* New York: Frederick A. Praeger, 1969.

Hirschman, Albert O., ed. *Latin American Issues.* New York: The Twentieth Century Fund, 1961.

———. *Journeys Toward Progress.* New York: The Twentieth Century Fund, 1963.

Krause, Walter, ed. *The Economy of Latin America.* University of Iowa: Bureau of Business and Economic Research, 1966.

Krause, Walter, and Mathis, F. John. *The Latin American Common Market: Economic Disparity and Benefit Diffusion.* Georgia State College: Bureau of Business and Economic Research, 1968.

Mathis, F. John. *Economic Integration in Latin America: The Problems and Progress of LAFTA.* University of Texas: Bureau of Business Research, 1969.

Mayobre, José Antonio et al. *Hacia la Integración Acelerada de América Latina.* Mexico City: Fondo de Cultura Económica, 1965.

Nye, Joseph S. *Central American Regional Integration.* New York: Carnegie Endowment for International Peace. 1967.

Olivos, Sergio Gutiérrez. *Subdesarrollo, Integración y Alianza.* Buenos Aires: Emecé Editores, 1963.

Ramsett, David E. *Regional Industrial Development in Central America.* New York: Frederick A. Praeger, 1969.

Teichert, Pedro C. *Revolución Económica e Industrialización en América Latina.* Mexico City: Fondo de Cultura Económica, 1963.

Urquidi, Victor L. *Free Trade and Economic Integration in Latin America.* Berkeley: University of California Press, 1962.

———. *The Challenge of Development in Latin America.* New York: Frederick A. Praeger, 1962.

Wionczek, Miguel S., ed. *La Integración de América Latina: Experiencias y Perspectivas.* Mexico City: Fondo de Cultura Económica, 1964.

———. *Latin American Free Trade Association.* New York: Carnegie Endowment for International Peace, 1965.

———, ed. *Latin American Economic Integration: Experiences and Prospects.* New York: Frederick A. Praeger, 1966.

———. *Economic Cooperation in Latin America, Africa, and Asia: A Handbook of Documents.* Cambridge: M.I.T. Press, 1969.

ARTICLES:

Baranson, Jack. "Industrialization and Regionalism in Central America." *Inter-American Economic Affairs,* Autumn 1962.

Brewster, J. Alan. "The Central American Program for Integrated Industrial Development." *Public and International Affairs,* Spring 1966.

Cochrane, James D. "U.S. Attitudes toward Central American Integration." *Inter-American Economic Affairs,* Autumn 1964.

Crow, John W. "Economic Integration in Central America." In International Monetary Fund (and IBRD), *Fund and Bank Review: Finance and Development,* March 1966.

Farag, Attiat A. "Economic Integration in Latin America." *Economia Internazionale,* November 1963.

Feder, Ernest. "Some Reflections on Latin America's Common Market." *The American Journal of Economics and Sociology,* July 1961.

Gonzalez del Valle, Jorge. "Monetary Integration in Central America: Achievements and Expectations." *Journal of Common Market Studies,* September 1966.

Huelin, David. "Economic Integration of Latin America—Progress and Problems." *International Affairs,* July 1964.

Labastida, Horacio. "Aspectos Sociales de la Integración Económica." *El Trimestre Económico,* January–March 1965.

Martirena de Mantel, Ana M. "Integración y Economías de Escala." *El Trimestre Económico,* July–September 1964.

Mitchell, Christopher. "Common Market: The Future of a Commitment —Punta del Este and After." *Inter-American Economic Affairs,* Winter 1967.

Navarrete, Jorge E. "Latin American Economic Integration—A Survey of Recent Literature." *Journal of Common Market Studies,* December 1965.

Perloff, Harvey S., and Almeida, Rómulo. "Regional Economic Integration in the Development of Latin America." *Economía Latinoamericana,* November 1963.

García Reynoso, Plácido. "Probables Efectos del Tratado de Montevideo en la Industrialización de América Latina." *El Trimestre Económico,* April–June 1960.

Staley, Charles E. "Central American Economic Integration." *The Southern Economic Journal,* October 1962.

Taylor, Benjamin J., and Bond, M. E. "Mexican Border Industrialization." *MSU Business Topics,* Spring 1968.

Wionczek, Miguel S. "EUA ante la Integración Económica de América Latina." In *La Integración Económica Latinoamericana,* Mexico City: Banco Nacional de Comercio Exterior, 1963.

DOCUMENTS:

Banco Nacional de Comercio Exterior, *Comercio Exterior,* Mexico City; monthly.

Centro de Estudios Monetarios Latinoaméricanos, *Actividad Económica en América Latina,* Mexico City; monthly.

________, *Boletín Quincenal,* Mexico City; monthly.

________, *Suplemento al Boletín Quincenal,* Mexico City; monthly.

ECLA–FAO, *The Role of Agriculture in the Latin American Common Market and Free-Trade Area Arrangements,* Santiago, 1961.

LAFTA, *Síntesis Mensual,* Montevideo; monthly.

Pincus, Joseph. *The Central American Common Market.* Washington: AID–ROCAP, 1962.

SIECA (Permanent Secretariat of the General Treaty of Central American Integration), *Carta Informativa,* Guatemala City; monthly.

———, *The Central American Common Market,* Guatemala City, December 1964.

United Nations, *The Latin American Common Market,* New York, 1959.

———, *Multilateral Economic Co-operation in Latin America* (Vol. I: Text and Documents), New York, 1962.

———, *Towards a Dynamic Development Policy for Latin America,* New York, 1963.

———, *The Economic Development of Latin America in the Post-War Period,* New York, 1964.

———, *The Process of Industrial Development in Latin America,* New York, 1966.

United Nations (UNCTAD), *Proposals for the Creation of the Latin American Common Market,* New York, 1965.

United Nations (ECLA), *Economic Survey of Latin America, 1965,* Santiago, 1967.

———, *The Economically Relatively Less Developed Countries and Latin American Integration,* New York, 1967.

Wardlaw, Andrew B. *The Operation of the Central American Common Market.* Guatemala City: AID–ROCAP, August 1966.

PLANNING

BOOKS:

Barna, Tibor, ed., in collaboration with Abraham, William I., and Kenessey, Zoltán. *Structural Interdependence and Economic Development* (Proceedings: International Conference on Input-Output Techniques, Geneva, 1961). New York: St. Martin's Press, 1963.

Hagan, Everett E., ed. *Planning Economic Development.* Homewood, Ill.: Richard D. Irwin, 1963.

Herbert, John D., and Van Huyck, Alfred P., eds. *Urban Planning in the Developing Countries.* New York: Frederick A. Praeger, 1968.

Hirschman, Albert O. *Development Projects Observed.* Washington: The Brookings Institution, 1967.

Hufschmidt, Maynard M., ed. *Regional Planning: Challenge and Prospects.* New York: Frederick A. Praeger, 1969.

Isard, Walter, and Cumberland, John H., eds. *Regional Economic Planning: Techniques of Analysis for Less Developed Areas.* Paris: European Productivity Agency of the Organization for European Economic Cooperation, 1961.

Lewis, W. Arthur. *Development Planning.* New York: Harper & Row, 1966.

Pontificia Academia Scientiarvm. *The Econometric Approach to Development Planning.* Amsterdam: North-Holland Publishing Company, 1965.

Walinsky, Louis J. *The Planning and Execution of Economic Development.* New York: McGraw-Hill Book Co., 1963.

Waterston, Albert. *Development Planning: Lessons of Experience.* Baltimore: Johns Hopkins Press, 1965.

Wolf, Charles, Jr., and Sufrin, Sidney C. *Capital Formation and Foreign Investment in Underdeveloped Areas: An Analysis of Research Needs and Program Possibilities Prepared from a Study Supported by the Ford Foundation.* Syracuse: Syracuse University Press, 1958.

ARTICLES:

Ashton, A. S. "Investment Planning by Private Enterprise." *Lloyd's Bank Review,* October 1962.

Baerresen, Donald W. "A Method for Planning Economic Integration for Specified Industries." *Journal of Common Market Studies,* September 1967.

Beechert, E. D. "The Gap Between Planning Goals and Achievements in Latin America." *Inter-American Economic Affairs,* Summer 1965.

Vernon, Raymond. "Comprehensive Model-building in the Planning Process: The Case of the Less-Developed Economies." *Economic Journal,* March 1966.

DOCUMENTS:

INTAL (Instituto Latinoamericano de Planificación Económica y Social), *Algunos Aspectos de la Incorporación de la Integración Económica a los Planes de Desarrollo,* Buenos Aires, February 1967.

OAS-IDB-ECLA (Misión Conjunta de Programación para Centroamérica), *Lineamientos para una Política de Desarrollo Regional,* Guatemala City, September 1964.

———, *Informe sobre el Resultado de la Coordinación Regional de los Inversiones Publicas,* Guatemala City, June 1965.

———, *Resultado de los Discusiones de los Programas Industriales Nacionales al Nivel Regional,* Guatemala City, August 1965.

———, *Informe de la Reunión Interinstitucional para Discutir el Documento: Bases para un Programa Centroamericano de Desarrollo Industrial,* Guatemala City, August 1966.

Pan American Union, *Informe sobre los Planes Nacionales de Desarrollo y el Proceso de Integración de Centroamérica,* Washington, August 1966.

United Nations, "Progress in Planning in Latin America," *Economic Bulletin for Latin America,* October 1963.

________, *Development Plans: Appraisal of Targets and Progress in Developing Countries,* New York, 1965.

FINANCE, BUSINESS, AND TRADE

BOOKS:

Baerresen, Donald W.; Carnoy, Martin; and Grunwald, Joseph. *Latin American Trade Patterns.* Washington: The Brookings Institution, 1965.

Blough, Roy; Behrman, Jack N.; and Ferrero, Rómulo A. *Regional Integration and the Trade of Latin America.* Washington: National Planning Association, 1968.

Brandenburg, Frank. *The Development of Latin American Private Enterprise.* Washington: National Planning Association, 1964.

Harrod, Roy, and Hague, Douglas C., eds. *International Trade Theory in a Developing World.* London: Macmillan Co., 1963.

Johnson, Harry G. *Economic Policies toward Less Developed Countries.* New York: Frederick A. Praeger, 1967.

König, Wolfgang. *Latin American Exchange-Rate Policies and the International Monetary Fund.* New York: Frederick A. Praeger, 1969.

Lauterbach, Albert. *Enterprise in Latin America: Business in a Developing Economy.* Ithaca: Cornell University Press, 1966.

Linder, Staffan B. *Comercio Internacional y Política Comercial para el Desarrollo.* Mexico City: Centro de Estudios Monetarios Latinoaméricanos, 1965.

Uri, Pierre; Kaldor, Nicholas; Ruggles, Richard; and Triffin, Robert. *A Monetary Policy for Latin America.* New York: Frederick A. Praeger, 1968.

Vernon, Raymond, ed. *How Latin America Views the U.S. Investor.* New York: Frederick A. Praeger, 1966.

Weintraub, Sidney. *Trade Preferences for Less-Developed Countries.* New York: Frederick A. Praeger, 1967.

ARTICLES:

Business International, Inc. *Business Latin America.* New York; various issues.

Herrera, Felipe. "The Inter-American Development Bank and the Latin American Integration Movement." *Journal of Common Market Studies,* December 1966.

Kessing, F. A. G., and Brand, P. J. "The Possible Role of a Clearing House in the Latin American Regional Market." In International Monetary Fund, *Staff Papers,* Washington, November 1963.

Márquez, Javier. "Coordinación de Políticas Monetarias en América Latina." In Centro de Estudios Monetarios Latinoaméricanos, *Coordinación Monetaria Regional,* Mexico City, 1963.

Tinbergen, Jan. "Heavy Industry in the Latin American Common Market." *Economic Bulletin for Latin America,* March 1960.

Triffin, Robert. "International Monetary Arrangements, Capital Markets and Economic Integration in Latin America." *Journal of Common Market Studies,* October 1965.

Turnage, W. V. "Unstable Currencies Hamper LAFTA Trade Growth." *International Commerce,* September 25, 1967.

DOCUMENTS:

Centro de Estudios Monetarios Latinoaméricanos, *Cooperación Financiera en América Latina,* Mexico City, 1963.

_______, *Problemas de Pagos en América Latina,* Mexico City, 1964.

Inter-American Development Bank, *Aspectos Financieros de la Integración Económica,* Caracas, April 1963.

_______, *Multinational Investment Programs and Latin American Integration,* New York, September 1966.

_______, *The Inter-American Development Bank and the Economic Integration of Latin America,* Washington, November 1966.

OAS (IA-ECOSOC), *Meeting of Government Representatives on the Financial Implications of Latin American Integration,* Washington: Pan American Union, 1968.

OAS–IDB, ECLA–Joint Tax Program, *Fiscal Policy for Economic Growth in Latin America,* Baltimore: Johns Hopkins Press, 1965.

Pan American Union, *Financing Economic Development in Latin America,* Washington, 1958.

United Nations (ECLA), *Latin America and the United Nations Conference on Trade and Development,* New York, 1964.

TRANSPORTATION AND COMMUNICATIONS

BOOKS:

Brown, Robert T. *Transport and the Economic Integration of South America.* Washington: The Brookings Institution, 1966.

Stokes, Charles J. *Transportation and Economic Development in Latin America.* New York: Frederick A. Praeger, 1968.

ARTICLES:

Angulo, Enrique. "El Transporte y el Comercio Interlatinoamericano." In *La Integración de América Latina: Experiencias y Perspectivas,* edited by Miguel S. Wionczek. Mexico City: Fondo de Cultura Económica, 1964.

Magariños de Mello, Mateo. "El Transporte Marítimo y la Asociación Latinoamericana de Libre Comercio," *El Trimestre Económico,* January–March 1965.